THE ULTIMATE BUSINESS TUNE UP

I have been working with Rich Allen for the past 3 years. My business would not be where it is today if it weren't for his direction and guidance. No matter what stage you are in your business or what business you are in, Rich puts everything business owners and entrepreneurs need to know in perspective in a metaphorical, easy to read text that I highly recommend!

—**Mike Hanna**, Owner, Investmark Mortgage, www.imhardmoney.com

Like many business owners and entrepreneurs, we often get caught up in wanting to do it OUR way and spend a lot of time re-inventing the wheel. The principles outlined in this book are the fundamentals you can't ignore. Rich has boiled down these concepts into digestible and easily actionable steps that allow any level of business owner to execute and create a business that works PROFITABLY!

—**Russel Dubree**, Founding Partner, Lifeblue, www.lifeblue.com

Starting a business as a young entrepreneur, Rich and his personal yet direct method of coaching could not have been more fitting and necessary. I think in part because of his own experiences and those of his father's, there wasn't much I could say that surprised or shocked him…and as a business owner, that was a relief. He's willing to get in the trenches with you while simultaneously ushering you to rise above—giving you confidence that "YES YOU CAN!" We are forever grateful for Rich and the support he has provided.

—**Katy Rogers**, Co-Owner, Stems of Dallas, www.stemsofdallas.com

The Ultimate Business Tune Up is a must read for all business owners as it really makes you stop and reflect on where you are going with your business. In it, Rich offers many practical suggestions on "looking ahead" and anticipating the future, which is often a huge challenge for business owners as we spend too much time on daily activities. Rich's advice on surrounding yourself with many advisors to lean on is excellent and a very practical way for business owners to weather the business challenges that come your way.

—**Scott Hutter**, Owner, Hutter Solutions, www.hutter.solutions

The Ultimate Business Tune-Up is like having your own business coach personally walk you through every facet of your business and make improvements. With it, you have the ability to take your business to the next level. Rich helps you create a grand vision for what you want your business to be as well as a systematic plan for getting there. Every entrepreneur should read this book!

—**Micah Grant**, Owner & CEO, Texas Stone Designs, Inc.
www.texasstonedesigns.com

When I started my HR Outsourcing business, I knew I was lacking the skills needed to grow successfully. With Rich's help, I built my management dashboard and learned how to look at my business in an entirely different way. The ideas and concepts outlined in this book have been an integral part of my success. With this guidance, I built a profitable company that I was able to sell!

—**Karen LaCroix**, Founder & President, MatchPoint HR,
www.matchpointhr.com

I'm a huge fan of learning from mistakes, and sometimes we can learn better from others' mistakes rather than our own. When I read Rich's story I became an immediate fan of his methodology and approach. I continue to rely on his coaching and am one of his biggest fans. I encourage everyone *who has ever thought about owning their own business,* as well as those *who actually own their own businesses,* to read this book and let Rich help you ride successfully and profitably!

—**Mike McCormack**, Founder and President, PeopleRight,
www.people-right.com

As a client and friend of Rich Allen, I have had the privilege of receiving this valuable insight first hand. Rich not only knows how to help a business grow, he genuinely wants to make a difference in the lives of business owners. He is one of the good guys! I highly recommend Rich and this book to any business owner looking to conquer the world.

—**Matt Bowman**, Founder and President,
Thrive Internet Marketing, www.thrivenetmarketing.com

In *The Ultimate Business Tune Up*, Rich draws from the lessons learned from his dad and proven experience to explain in easy-to-read, easy-to-understand language how to manage a business. He distinguishes the critical difference between being an expert in a chosen field or craft and running a business, and he provides the tools needed by both entrepreneurs and long-time business owners to plan, manage and measure a successful company.

—**Chris Johnson**, Owner and Publisher,
Style Publishing Group, www.friscostyle.com

What business doesn't need a tune up from time to time? Rich is providing the readers of his new book with sound business advice as well as the processes needed to reach the next level in building a successful business. Readers get a peek into Rich's background to learn what motivated him so strongly to help businesses not only survive but also to thrive. The information provided in the chapters on "Self-Assessment" and "Life Balance" is rarely touched on by business books but is so important.

—**John Health**, President, Lone Star Benefits, Inc., www.lsbinc.com

Over five years I relied upon Rich's expertise and guidance to make the necessary changes in my business that I could not make on my own. Rich possesses an innate ability to prompt clients to approach change from an unanticipated perspective. He leads the client through the change process with logic and insight drawing upon his personal experience in the corporate world and years of business coaching. Rich and I have grown to be friends over five years of coaching and consulting, which speaks to the quality of his character both personally and professionally.

—**Brendan Bass**, Owner, Brendan Bass Showroom, www.brendanbass.com

Rich Allen has done a masterful job of telling the story of how to achieve greater success in your life and business. *The Ultimate Business Tune Up* is extremely well written, enjoyable to read, and very touching with great lessons and stories from his life experiences with his father.

—**Paul O. Williams**, CEO, Bison Financial Group, Inc.,
www.bisonfinancialgroup.com

If you're ready to take your business to the next level, this is the perfect book for you. Whether you are a "one-man-band" doing it all or an organization with 100 employees, the content is relevant, and Rich Allen's delivery is straight-forward and on target. The parallels in the book are very impactful and reinforce the key points. Having utilized most of Rich's methodologies, I've been able to streamline my entire business, increase profits to double-digit numbers, form a winning team with unbelievable morale and drive, and most importantly, have more time to spend with my family and friends. Thank you Rich Allen!

—**Michelle Young**, Co-Owner, Legacy Plumbing, www.legacyplumbing.net

Starting and growing a successful business is not for the faint of heart. Praise God there is now a solid road map to help start and keep your business on the right track. *The Ultimate Business Tune Up* is a must read for any entrepreneur who is committed to "achieving success the right way" by working smarter not harder. Rich uses his Dad's experiences in running a struggling family business to illustrate this point. His proven philosophy and processes layout the steps he has learned to run a businesses and provide valuable advice on how to reduce risk and improve chances for sustainability and profitable growth. Whether you are a seasoned rider or still have your training wheels on, you will enjoy this ride with Rich!

—**Jay Arntzen**, Founder and President, Genesis Elevator Company, Inc., www.genesiselevator.com

THE ULTIMATE
BUSINESS
TUNE UP

A Simple Yet Powerful Business Model
That Will Transform the Lives of
SMALL BUSINESS OWNERS

RICH ALLEN

NEW YORK

NASHVILLE MELBOURNE

THE ULTIMATE BUSINESS TUNE UP
A Simple Yet Powerful Business Model That Will Transform the Lives of SMALL BUSINESS OWNERS

Published in New York, New York, by Morgan James Publishing. Morgan James and The Entrepreneurial Publisher are trademarks of Morgan James, LLC. www.MorganJamesPublishing.com

The Morgan James Speakers Group can bring authors to your live event. For more information or to book an event visit The Morgan James Speakers Group at www.TheMorganJamesSpeakersGroup.com.

Shelfie

A **free** eBook edition is available with the purchase of this print book.

ISBN 978-1-68350-057-5 paperback
ISBN 978-1-68350-059-9 eBook
ISBN 978-1-68350-058-2 hardcover
Library of Congress Control Number:
2016906924

CLEARLY PRINT YOUR NAME ABOVE IN UPPER CASE

Instructions to claim your free eBook edition:
1. Download the Shelfie app for Android or iOS
2. Write your name in **UPPER CASE** above
3. Use the Shelfie app to submit a photo
4. Download your eBook to any device

Cover Design by:
Rachel Lopez
www.r2cdesign.com

Interior Design by:
Bonnie Bushman
The Whole Caboodle Graphic Design

In an effort to support local communities, raise awareness and funds, Morgan James Publishing donates a percentage of all book sales for the life of each book to Habitat for Humanity Peninsula and Greater Williamsburg.

Get involved today! Visit
www.MorganJamesBuilds.com

To my Dad:
Who taught me everything I know,
Showed me how to work hard,
Demonstrated the meaning of "never quit,"
And blessed me with the will
To always reach high.

TABLE OF CONTENTS

ACKNOWLEDGEMENTS

I want to extend my sincere appreciation and thanks to several people who were instrumental in bringing this book to life.

First and foremost, I want to thank my family whom I love very much and who have supported me through all of my crazy ideas and business ventures. My wife, Drew, is my steady rock and my kids, Megan, Rhett and Anne Drew provide the motivation to charge forward every day.

I am blessed to have eleven brothers and sisters who each have a story worth sharing. We struggled through our younger years together and while we may have grown apart over time, I still love them deeply and wish for them only the very best.

A huge shout out to my clients, many of whom have become good friends along the way and who inspire me with their courageous efforts to make their businesses successful and convert that success into significance.

This book would never have seen the light of day without the tireless efforts of my editor, Clark Waggoner, and his behind the scenes team. Clark put up with several direction changes, format revisions and meticulous details, and for that I can only say thank you from the bottom of my heart.

My transcription specialist, Clarissa Chiu, was at the very beginning of this project and without her efforts, this book would never have always just been a "someday" project. Thank you for your hard work Clarissa!

There were many others who inspired me along the way and to each of you (you know who you are) I want to say thanks.

And finally, the biggest thanks to my Lord and Savior Jesus Christ. I have been truly blessed to have this father, live this life and be able to share this story. I owe it all to him, every day.

INTRODUCTION

On May 29, 2013, the inevitable happened. The culmination of 77 years of hard work, determination, personal triumphs and gut-wrenching defeats finally came to an end. It didn't happen like it does in Hollywood, but that didn't come as a surprise. What we'd hoped for was that it would happen suddenly and peacefully, without any pain. Turns out that was the case.

The days just before proved the most difficult for those of us closest to him. Eleven brothers and sisters gathered at the house for the first time since Mom died some 20 years earlier, returning now to decide whether or not to take Dad off life support.

It wasn't easy. Some in the room hadn't spoken to one another for years. Decades of pain, frustration, resentment, and anger had to be overcome or overlooked just to sit down with each other. The living room was small—too small to hold all of the emotions we siblings brought with us as we slowly arrived. Some sat quietly, not making eye contact with anyone. Others fondly greeted aging kin they hadn't seen in years.

Why does it take a tragedy to bring loved ones together? Why must someone die to bring a family together? Shouldn't we want to share good times with one another instead of just seeing each other during times of loss?

Once everyone arrived, the eldest son assumed the role of mediator. He had the thankless task of getting this unlikely board of directors to somehow reach consensus on what should happen next. Do we keep Dad on life support or take him off? If he survives, does he go into a nursing home or go live with one of us? How do we cover his hospital bills? It was a daunting if not impossible task.

But instead of stalemate, *a small miracle happened*—the kind that often do when least expected. Despite all the pent-up emotion, and perhaps even a little venom in the room, one by one, everyone agreed together to do what was right—to put aside any differences and make the best decisions possible for our father. When it mattered most, the important task of doing what Dad would have wanted somehow overcame the years of baggage and bitterness that had grown between us children.

So that's what we did. Through tears, each sibling shared his or her feelings, thoughts and beliefs. It was hard for many, but once the emotional door was open, each of us was able to walk through it and open up about why we felt so strongly about our opinion. And even though Dad was in a coma in a hospital 10 miles away, he was in that room with us, watching and listening to each one of his children share what he had taught them over his many years of living.

The decision was unanimous—each and every son and daughter, on their own, came to the conclusion that they knew Dad would not want to be on life support. Yes, this unity was a miracle, but the bigger miracle that happened in that room was the healing between the siblings that took place. Years of issues couldn't simply be resolved in one meeting, but the emotions, feelings, and thoughts that were shared brought each of us closer to one another than we had been since childhood. I consider this just one more gift from the man who had been a teacher to us all throughout our lives.

We took Dad off life support 5 days later and he finally left us. But not before he awoke from the coma one last time—to the amazement of the doctors. For just a brief 20 seconds, Dad came out of his coma, looked into the eyes of my brother as he captured the event on video, smiled and told us he loved us all and that he was ready to be with his wife. Before he passed, he made sure to let us know we'd made the right decision and that he'd be waiting for us patiently in heaven.

Dad is with our Mother now. They are finally reunited and enjoying the peace that only God can provide. Thanks be to God. My father left a legacy that his 12 children can be proud of, and one that I hope to share a bit more with you over the course the of his book.

My father's teachings were not always direct, positive, and by-example. In fact, many times he taught us from a distance and by demonstrating what NOT to do. But what is certain is that his children were watching, observing, listening and interpreting his every move throughout his life. He was the teacher and we were the students. And the more I think about it, the more I understand what he was trying to teach us.

As I share these lessons and stories about my father with you in this book, I hope to impart a bit of the wisdom I learned from his examples. I hope the lessons and stories of my father will resonate with you, compel you to greater success in your life and business, and help you learn as I did from his life experiences.

Chapter 1

MY DAD,
THE BUSINESS OWNER

EARLY LIFE & STARTING A BUSINESS

Most of the messes and difficulties that we get ourselves into are of our own making. This was certainly the case with my father. He didn't have to look far to find someone to blame for the situations he found himself in because he could clearly see the culprit in the mirror every single morning.

From the very beginning, he penned his own script. He met Patricia when he was a teenager. His first major decision was to get married before finishing high school—a decision that would set their lives set off on a financially difficult and emotionally challenging path.

Not long after getting married, they were already expecting their first child. Though they were both teenagers and hardly prepared to be parents, they bravely stepped up. With the birth of their first son on Christmas Eve, 1953, their new life was now a reality.

A Growing Young Family

Over the next several years, it must have seemed as if his wife was constantly pregnant. Next came a second son, then a daughter, then another son, followed by another daughter. Now with five children and barely 25 years old, they had to move to a bigger home to fit their growing family.

Neither this move nor child would be their last. A rhythm of pregnancy & childbirth, pregnancy & childbirth would continue along with the parallel rhythm of settling in & moving, settling in & moving. As the family grew, so did their need for greater income.

Dad never faltered in his commitment to supporting his growing family, though he didn't have a high school education which severely limited his options. It wasn't long before a single labor job was insufficient to meet his family's financial needs. Something had to give. Without complaint, he simply did what he had to and got another job.

Setting An Example Of Taking Responsibility

I must admit that as a young boy, I was mostly unaware of the hardships and financial frustrations my mom and dad faced. To me, it was just the way things were. I was used to eating fish sticks and spam for dinner and playing with sticks, old card board, and rocks. I do remember my parents arguing from time to time, but I never saw my dad back away from his responsibilities. He was responsible for this family and he was going to do whatever was necessary to make ends meet.

This is uncommon today. Unfortunately, we too often hear about parents who find themselves facing difficulties and just give up or look for a hand out rather than a hand up. But that was not my dad. The way he saw things, the only option he had for taking care of a house full of kids was to work his tail off until the ends met. Instead of government assistance, he relied on conviction and determination, and he never complained of how hard he had to work.

Sure, there may have been an easier path to follow, but what I learned from my dad was that nothing beat hard work and determination. It may not solve all problems, but if you're going to stand a chance, you'd better be ready to work as hard as you can all day, every day. So it's no surprise that my dad set out with this mindset when he decided to become a small business owner.

MY DAD AS A BUSINESS OWNER

When Dad finally decided to start his own business, he was already working *at least* two jobs a week. He had his regular job during the day, his night job at the factory, and also all the odd jobs he could find on the weekends. For my father, life was a grind. Every day was a struggle. This grind led him, at age 38, to make the most difficult decision of his life—he quit his regular job to start his own full-time business.

You see, my dad had a dream. He had a vision. He wanted to build a business and leave a legacy for his eight sons. The proudest day of his life was when he took his used van, stenciled lettering on the sides (pictured on the back cover), and started his own window washing business. My dad was, without a doubt, the *best* window washer imaginable—extremely detailed and hardworking. He was an expert at his chosen trade. But he had one major challenge; my dad had no clue how to run a business.

A Typical Day On The Job

A work day for my dad went like this: he'd wake up very early, get ready for work, then sit in his van and flip through his Big Chief tablets where he kept his customer lists. He'd write down the names of those he was going to work for that day and go wash their windows. They'd always be thrilled with his work, but invariably, his disorganization led him to forget one or more customers he'd promised to do work for that day, and they would be very disappointed.

Each day started out as a struggle. Without any processes in place, he failed to do key tasks like ensure his equipment was ready which led to continually chaotic starts to the day. Furthermore, because my dad was good at everything, he *did* everything, so he never would focus on any one thing. If someone asked him to do something, he would do it and do it very well, but he failed to focus on what he was BEST at and rarely sat down to plan out his work.

Mismanaging Business Finances

Dad didn't manage his finances very well either. In fact, he didn't even have a bank account! He was often paid in cash, but occasionally his customers gave him a check. When he got paid with a check, he had nowhere to cash it besides the local bar.

After finishing work each day, he'd often have to stop at the local bar to cash his checks. They'd be glad to cash them so long as he bought something. This was no problem for my dad who would have himself a well-deserved beer. But one led to two, and two led to three or more. Often, the day's earnings were spent at the bar while his family was waiting at home needing some money to buy groceries for dinner. On many nights, dinner never came and the family went to bed hungry.

On a couple of occasions, he came home late only to find his family and their belongings on the curb, having been evicted because he hadn't paid the bills. So he'd empty the van of work gear, fill it with our furniture and set out to find a new place for the family to live.

Despite all this, my dad was an optimist. He'd repeat to himself and all of us, "Someday, we'll get this right. If we just work hard enough, things will get better." But sadly, that day never came.

Losing The Support Of His Family

One by one, his sons became frustrated working with him and decided they could find better work elsewhere. One at a time, they left. One of his sons even decided he could run a window washing business better than his Dad and started his own competing business. His wife, growing tired of the grind and his continual belief that "the dream" was still out there, finally, after 30 years of marriage, said, "I've had enough" and asked for a divorce.

But my dad didn't quit. He didn't know how. He just kept plugging away, believing that one day, if he just worked hard enough, his dreams would come true. But they never did…

MY JOURNEY AND HOW IT LED ME TO WRITING THIS BOOK

One of his sons got very lucky. He received a scholarship to go to college that allowed him to leave home for the first time and travel over 1500 miles away. After graduation, he joined the military for a time. After a successful stint in the military, he landed a very nice corporate job. Because he was a hard worker like his Dad, he rose quickly through the corporate ranks and was soon running a fairly large business himself. This success allowed him to retire from his corporate job at the young age of 50.

That son then moved his family to Texas where he made the decision to commit the rest of his working life to helping business owners like his dad avoid the pitfalls, frustrations and problems that he watched his dad make.

Chapter 2

MY JOURNEY AS
A BUSINESS OWNER

I f you can't tell by now, let me be very clear, *I love my dad*. I learned a lot from him. He taught me everything he knew. But he had *no clue* how to run a business. And at the time, I didn't know how to help him. Not a day goes by that I don't wish I could turn the clock back and spend more time working with my dad. But it's too late. There's no going back. His recent passing inspired me to see the writing of this book through. That's why I'm writing these words today.

The memory of my dad's business failure drives me every day. It's what motivates me to get up in the morning. It's what makes me so excited to work with small, family-based business owners. I want them to have a different experience than my dad. I want *this* to be the legacy that I leave in honor of my father.

RUNNING A BUSINESS IS DIFFERENT THAN MASTERING A TRADE

Forget that my dad was the best window washer you could find. He had no clue how to run a business. What I've come to realize is that *it doesn't matter how good you are at your trade*. That's *not* what's going to make you successful in business. I see it so often. Too often, people are extraordinarily good (or even the best) at their trade, but they have no clue how to turn that into a profitable, sustainable business.

I believe that what's missing for many small business owners today is a fundamental underlying model they can follow that will allow them to *focus on the things that matter most* to their long-term business success. You see, focus is what's lacking in today's world—particularly for business owners. I believe my dad was missing this underlying model of how a business works which meant he had no clue *what to focus on or in what order.*

A TESTED AND PROVEN BUSINESS MODEL
FOR SMALL BUSINESS OWNERS

Over the past several years, I've worked on the business model I'll be sharing with you in this book. I've tested and measured it with hundreds of small business owners, and I believe now is the right time to share it with business owners like yourself. I truly believe you'll find this business model to be exactly what you're missing in your business today or I wouldn't waste your time. It's powerful, centering, and helps you tune out the noise and really focus on what matters most.

Now, you're probably in one of three places with your business right now:

1. **You recently launched your business.** This is an exciting but also scary time. If this is you, I believe my model may be just what you need to get off to a fast start.
2. **You have been in business for a while and it's not performing as you'd hoped.** If this is you, I believe that you'll find you're missing something my model will help you identify and implement into your business right away—a real difference maker.
3. **You've been in business a long time and are doing quite well, but feel you've plateaued and don't know how to reach the next level.** If this sounds like you, I believe my model can help you uncover exactly what it will take to grow your business like you've never seen before.

I truly believe in this model and it's power. I've seen it work again and again. But before we get started, I have a few questions I'd like you to think about:

1. *What do you struggle with the most in your business?*
2. *What takes your focus off the things that matter most?*
3. *Which of the three categories above is your business in?*

Once you've considered these questions for your specific business, you'll have the right frame of mind to address the issues and avoid the mistakes that overwhelmed my dad. So I encourage you to answer these questions for yourself before moving on.

THE ORIGINS OF THE MODEL

As I mentioned, I developed this model, specifically to help business owners like you. I've thought about it a lot, and what I put in this model is exactly what my dad was missing. So let's talk about the model a bit, starting with how I came up with it in a moment of desperation!

The Beginning Of The Model: Desperation Begets Inspiration

I was working for a large, privately-held manufacturing firm in a functional role, but I always had this idea that I wanted to run my own business. So I asked my boss, the CEO, if someday he would let me run one of our business units. His response was, "Sure Rich! Let's make the business work for now and then see how it goes."

Fast forward two years, my boss walks into my office and literally hands me the keys, saying, "Rich, congratulations, this one is yours." We had just purchased a small manufacturing company that had been operating poorly. The previous owner hadn't modernized the business so it wasn't currently profitable at all.

But, it was *my first real opportunity* to try my hand at running a business! As you can imagine, it was to me a "chance of a lifetime," something I've always wanted. So I was excited, but then I panicked because I realized I had no idea how I was going to improve the business.

Taking A Cue From My Father

But, like my dad, I was determined to do whatever it took to take advantage of this opportunity. So I moved my family to where the business was located and started a new chapter in my career. I went to the factory and walked around as if I knew what I was doing, but all the while I was thinking to myself, *what in the world have you gotten yourself into? What are you going to do now?* I had no clue.

For days, in fact weeks, I simply walked around the factory, talking to people, learning a little bit about what they were doing and trying to understand how the business worked. The whole time I was thinking, *how am I going to figure this out? What's going to make sense?* I believed, like my dad, that if I just kept working at it, I would come up with something. But the days were slipping by and I was becoming desperate.

That's when it hit me—in the morning shower of all places: at that time it was just the seed of an idea, but already I knew I was on to something. Over the next several days and weeks, I made notes and developed the idea. The more I thought, the more it made sense. Finally, it was time to act. I called my assistant and said, "Schedule a meeting with the whole team, I have something to share with everyone."

Chapter 3

THE FIRST MEETING
& BIKE AS A BUSINESS

W e had over 200 employees, so we cleared out a large section of the warehouse for an all-hands-on-deck meeting. We squeezed everyone in, and once assembled, I started to share my thoughts. But I didn't get in front of my team unprepared. I'd brought a bike and had it standing on a table beside me. Then I pointed to the bike and asked, "What's this?"

As you can imagine, I received some strange looks. Some people responded, "It's a bike," while others, unsure what was going on, responded with answers like "stolen property." We laughed and I assured them it wasn't stolen. But, then I said, "This isn't just a bike. This is our business."

Now this puzzled them. I could see questioning glances and raised eyebrows. I could hear them thinking to themselves, *Holy Cow! Who'd they send us this time? This guy's off his rocker!* I went on:

"This bike represents our business. I believe if we can all understand this, then we can figure out how to turn our business into the kind of bike that goes really fast."

Some heads nodded, a few were with me. So I took them on a tour of the bike to show them what I meant. They were starting to suspect I might have a point, so they played along. The tour I took them on is the same one I'd like to take you on in this book. At its core, my business model built upon the comparison between a bike and a business. That's right! The very business you are working on and concerned about today—*we're going to discuss for the rest of the book as if your business was a bike!*

Before we go in-depth, let's do a brief version of the tour so you have a good idea of *where* we'll be going and *why* throughout our journey together in this book.

THE BIKE AS A BUSINESS MODEL

The Handle Bars

On your bike you steer with your handlebars. In a business, you steer with *a vision*. You steer by painting a *CLEAR and COMPELLING* picture of where you want your business to go. The more passionate you are, the more motivated your people will be to follow. In most businesses, no one talks about the future or what they want the business to look like in 5 to 10 years. With no idea of where they are headed, how can people be excited about getting there? To fix this, you need to grab the handle bars and steer your business.

The Frame

The frame on the bike is what holds everything together. It gives your bike structure and strength. The frame of your business is what gives it structure and strength to last a long time. It includes *formal business documents like your legal agreements, operating documents and an exit plan.* It also includes *your organizational structure* and *all documents that inform team members of their primary job responsibilities and how they fit in your business.* If it's not clear who does what, things fall through the cracks and customers will be less than completely satisfied with your service.

Everything must connect. You must be very clear about (1) who does what, (2) how handoffs occur, and (3) how processes connect to one another. Without a good solid frame in your business, it becomes wobbly and you'll never be able to go fast with it.

The Front Wheel

The front and back wheels of a bike are the two parts where the rubber actually meets the road. If you ever hope to go anywhere with your business, you must have two parts where the rubber literally meets the road—where you get good traction and grip that drives your business forward. Your business's **front wheel** is your process for winning new customers. It is made up of three components. (1) the hub, (2) the spokes, and (3) the tire:

> **The Hub:** This represents your avatar or ideal customer. You need to be extremely clear on who you're really trying to serve. Who is your perfect customer? You *must* know their needs, wants, and desires *intimately* to speak directly to them.
>
> **The Spokes:** Your spokes are *marketing strategies* or how you get your message to your ideal customer/avatar. With only 1–2 spokes, your front wheel will break. Your business needs 5–6 solid strategies, or spokes, providing a consistent flow of leads so you can grow.
>
> **The Tire:** The tire represents your sales process or how you get traction with those responding to your marketing messages. This is a step-by-step process that makes prospects so comfortable with you that they pull out their wallet and do business with you.

The Back Wheel

The back wheel is where power is generated. It is the engine that drives the bike faster. Your business's back wheel is how you deliver to your customers on the promises you made on the front wheel. You must not only deliver on the promise, but *over-deliver* to get rave reviews.

To do this, you need solid tread, or processes, within your business to deliver on your commitments. You need a solid delivery and service process that always works well no matter whether it's early Monday morning or late Friday afternoon. This is achieved by having good solid processes on the back wheel of your business.

On your bike, it's critical that your front and back wheels spin at the same speed. If they are spinning at different speeds, then something bad is going to happen. The same is true for your business. So it is critical that both the front and back wheels of your business have the capacity to turn at the same speed.

The Brakes & Indicators

When it comes to keeping both wheels on your business moving at the same speed, you do it the same way you do on your bike, with brakes. In business, brakes are *your financial controls*. They're what you use to determine whether you need to slow down on spending on your marketing and sales (front wheel) or production and operations (back wheel) of your business.

On a well-built bike, there is a device that mounts to your handlebars that shows your speed, distance traveled, incline, and maybe even heart rate. In business, those same kinds of indicators help you track performance and look ahead. These are called *Key Performance Indicators (KPIs)*. These kinds of indicators will help you predict *how your business is likely to perform in the future*. Without them, it is difficult to tell how well your business is doing.

The Seat

Now the seat on a bike is pretty important. I don't have to tell you how uncomfortable it is to get on a bike if the seat is not positioned well, broken, or unstable. It's not only frustrating, it can be dangerous. The seat must be *securely positioned in a way that allows maximum power to be delivered to the pedals.*

In your business, the seat is where the people who are going to be pushing the pedals of your business sit. You need them positioned well to allow them to really propel your business forward. This includes people programs like *your compensation plan, reward systems, communication plan, incentive programs, and recognition programs.* These programs will determine how comfortable your seat is. When your seat is properly positioned, your team will work hard day after day to help you achieve your goals.

Can you see it now? How a bike really is a business? Crazy, right? A bike is a perfect metaphor for a business. We can use it to understand the different parts of your business and how they work together. And just like a bike, if any part of your business is broken, it's no fun to ride.

HOW THE BIKE MODEL TRANSFORMED OUR BUSINESS

So I shared this story with my team and immediately people started coming up and saying, "Rich, I think I know what's wrong with our business." One-by-one they started relating the business different parts of our bike. *They got it!* They could really start to see how different aspects of the bike related to different aspects of our business.

Fast-forward seven years later, we were five times larger and very profitable. We were a player in the marketplace—we owned the top end product categories. Then, as is often the case, our largest competitor came to us and made an offer to buy the company. We negotiated a good deal, I made sure that our people were taken care of, and I was able to retire at age 50!

I took some time off to spend with my family and be a real dad. Then, prompted by answers to our prayers, we moved to Texas and I committed the rest of my professional career to helping small business owners like yourself understand how you can take your business, tune it up, and make it go faster than you ever thought possible. That's what I've done in my mentoring program, my online program, and now, finally, in *this* book.

Since moving to Texas, I've written two books, worked with hundreds of business owners, facilitated numerous strategy sessions, and helped start up a half-dozen small businesses using the bike model I just described.

I believe in this model and have seen it work incredibly well time and time again. Perhaps you're already able to identify some areas in your own business based on this model. Starting to get some ideas of what might "be broken" or need "tuning up" in your business? I hope you can see why so many business owners are excited about using this model. If so, it only gets better from here as we focus specifically on the different elements of a highly detailed blueprint you can use to improve any aspect of your business in need of a tune up.

TUNE-UP TIP: Organize your thoughts from this chapter by making a list of any parts of your "business/bike" you feel might need a tune-up. Keep this list in mind as you proceed through the book so you can make notes or add to it.

SECTION ONE

YOU, THE BUSINESS OWNER

Chapter 4

YOUR ROLE AS A
BUSINESS OWNER

L et's start at the top with *you, the business owner.* As the business owner, you are the single most important person in your business. *You* set the example and the standards. How *you behave*, others follow. So we want to make sure that your head is positioned in the right place to lead your business successfully.

Reality check. The bottle neck for your business will always be *you*, the owner. So the first thing you must do is *expand the top-end capabilities of your business. That is, expand what you yourself are able to do for your business.* That's the focus in this section—going over several important aspects and getting your mind right so you can find the time and create the energy your business needs to thrive.

MY DAD AS A BUSINESS OWNER

As we take this journey together, we'll stop and check in with my dad from time to time to see what we can learn from his example. As I mentioned before, he was always teaching his kids—even if these lessons weren't presented in the best way. I think he has a few lessons for you as a business owner as well. I'd like to share one of these relating to our discussion of being a business owner.

Once Dad made the decision to start his own small business, he never thought about himself. He was just "off and running." From that very first moment, he *knew* it was up to him to earn money to take care of his family and pay his bills. So he did what most small business owners do—*he jumped right in and started working.*

My dad was convinced that the primary ingredients to success were *hard work and commitment.* Success to him would come if he never showed weakness, never got tired, and never took a break. So he created these habits:

Get up before dawn and leave the house before anyone else wakes up. Drive an hour to the neighborhood he was going to work in, hit it hard all morning with no breaks, grab a quick lunch—normally while still working—and then get in several more jobs before it was time to quit at 6 pm or later. Then, back into the van, drive an hour home, arrive after dark, sit at the kitchen table sorting out the day's paperwork, and fall into bed dead tired by 11 pm—only to do it again the next day.

One of my dad's big mistakes was *never taking time to think* or *plan.* My dad had no life balance. He made no effort to talk to anyone with experience running a business. In his mind, it was most important that he *work*—not think, plan, rest, or get advice.

My dad's approach reminds me of the story of two guys who each had 1 hour to cut down a tree. The first guy grabbed his saw, ran to the tree and started cutting away. He worked very hard, pushing and pulling his saw as fast as he could and before long tired out.

Meanwhile, the other guy sat down and started sharpening his saw. He worked on sharpening his saw for 45 minutes making sure it was very, very sharp. Once it was ready, he cut the tree down with ease and with time to spare.

My dad was the first guy. Not a day goes by where I don't wish I would have known to advise him to be the second guy! So the point of this section is to help you find a moment to stop, think, and plan so you don't end up collapsing asleep dead tired every night with nothing to show for it like my dad.

TUNE-UP TIP: One interesting thing about balance is that you only really think about or sense it when it's gone. This means you need to be on your toes, so you know when you're starting to slip out of balance. We'll cover several strategies on how to do this throughout this section.

So with this in mind, let's ride!

Chapter 5

A SELF-ASSESSMENT

I n this chapter, we're going to talk about *your personal life goals*. Remember, your business is not a *goal*, but a *tool*. However, it needs to be a *major tool* that can truly help you achieve the life you've always wanted. That's why we're talking about goals up front, otherwise we'll have no criteria by which to assess your business as a tool.

This is something that my dad struggled with. My dad lived as if his life should revolve around his business. *Everything* was focused on it. As a result, he missed out on a lot of things going on around him that make life worth living. You see, while obsessing over his business, my dad missed out on the thrill of living, and you don't want to make that same mistake!

CREATING YOUR "LIFE CIRCLE"

For this first exercise I've included the image on the next page.

Now, we're all a little different, so our priorities will vary slightly. But for the most part, we can break them down into the categories on the circle above: *(1) relationships, (2) health & fitness, (3) finances, (4) spirituality, (5) education, (6) adventure,* and *(7) community.*

Number eight is for you to define on your own. You likely have something that doesn't neatly fall into these seven categories. Go ahead and write this in for

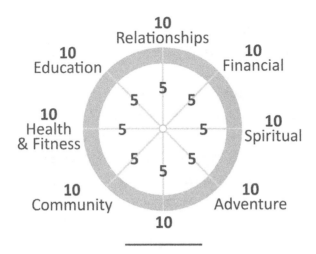

your eighth spoke. Take a moment to think about what's most important today and use that or simply leave it blank until something comes to you.

The center of the circle where the spokes meet represents "I'm lousy at achieving these goals" or a 1 on a scale of 1–10. The outside edge of the circle represents "I'm very successful at achieving these goals" or a 10 on a scale of 1–10. The outer circle symbolizes a perfect life with a 10 out of 10 in every category. Now let's talk about how to rate yourself:

Step One: Rating Yourself In Different Areas

Start by asking yourself, *where am I today?* Do this for each area on the circle. Ask yourself, *where do I honestly stand on this? How good of a job am I doing? Is it okay? Not-so-good? Genuinely great?* For some examples, on *Health & Fitness*, how happy you are with your current fitness level and life style? For education, *are you reading as much as you want?* Etc.

Do this for each category. *Does your family have the money it needs to realize your long term plans? Are you genuinely happy with the amount of time you get to spend with them?* I know for myself that I spend a lot of time in my business and frankly, that means I don't have as much time as I'd like to do exciting things with my family.

Your circle will look different from anyone else—even your spouse or your business partner. But realize that having a different circle isn't a big deal. We all excel at and are challenged by different things. Use the circle to focus on where *you* are today, that's what matters.

Step Two: Connecting The Dots

Once you've finished plotting, *connect the dots*. Now you have a visual representation of your progress in all the important areas of your life. Study your circle. *This is what your life looks like.* Instantly you should see areas that are particularly far behind or ahead and begin to assess how to achieve better balance. Take time and reflect on what your circle tells you.

Step Three: What You Want Your Circle To Look Like

Now think six months down the line. Imagine you make the improvements you want. You'll probably only have time to focus on one or two over the next six months. So the key is to *focus on the areas that need the most improvement.* Remember, we're talking about *life*, not *business*. Business is a tool, so you need to know how to use it which means your *life* comes first.

That's why it's *vitally important* you are honest during your assessment. You only hurt yourself if you are not. If it's *finances,* make that your goal. If you are *stuck in the grind,* find a way to get some adventure. If it's *fitness,* commit to a routine. Maybe you could even combine a couple?

 TUNE-UP TIP: As you assess your circle, you might start to realize that there are two or three areas that make sense to work on together so that you can maximize your efforts across multiple spokes.

Step Four: Mapping Out Your Six-Month Plan

Next, make a list of what you intend to do over the next six months about these things. Write these down so you can check in with them. Just record the actions you're going to take over the next six months to get a little bit better in each area.

With *Health & Fitness,* you could get up half an hour earlier each morning for a jog or run. Whatever it is, do something that will make *genuine incremental improvement.* So start where you are and *be realistic.* No idea is too small or unrealistic. Write them down; each step counts.

S.P.A.M. GOALS

When you write goals, think about them in in terms of *SPAM.* You see, SPAM was a part of my diet growing up. It was what I thought of when I thought of meat. Some people ate bologna, or hamburgers, but we ate SPAM. So that's always helped this concept stick in my head.

This SPAM is different. This SPAM is an acronym for setting goals where:

S—Specific: Your goal must be *specific.* This makes it easier to attain and measure.

P—Personal: Your goal must be *personal.* It needs to be attached to a person, in this case, *you.* It's *your* goal, so it must mean something to *you.*

A—Actionable: Your goal must be *actionable.* It needs to require you do something. A goal can't be to *think* about something. It must be *doing something* or *making something happen.*

M—Measurable: Your goal must be *measurable.* It needs a timeframe so that you can know if you accomplish it. For example, if your goal is to have a regular date night with your spouse, then *put it on the calendar!*

So SPAM your goals! Be **Specific, Personal, Actionable**, and **Measurable** as you go about achieving them. Do this *with every goal you set* as you work through this book.

CREATE ACCOUNTABILITY FOR YOUR GOALS

Now once you have your goals for the next six-months written out, *share them with somebody you trust* (like your spouse or business partner). Whoever you choose, ask them to hold you accountable.

We'll talk more about accountability later, but for right now, tell them, "I'm committed to making my life better so I can make my business better." That's the goal here.

The bottom line is this: when any of the areas on this wheel are not where they need to be, your performance in every area of your life will be negatively impacted. If this is true of your personal situation, *how much more true is it of your business?*

 TUNE-UP TIP: If you're like most business owners I know, when one of these areas is out of whack in your life, it saps your energy and focus. You can't concentrate on your business because your mind is pre-occupied. Just think of the last time you were worried about money to see how true this is. Worries over these areas consume our minds. So before we can ever look at your business, we first need to clear your mind of anything that may sap your focus or energy away from your efforts there.

Let's review:

1. Assess where you are today in the 8 most important areas of your life.
2. Create your own circle to visually represent your current progress in these areas.
3. Assess which 2–3 areas need the most improvement.
4. Implement a six-month plan to improve the areas that most need it.

Remember, this assessment is a tool to *help you.* You must be honest if you want to improve. So please, ask yourself, *where do you most want or need to make at least some improvement?* Take this seriously because it's vital for what comes next. Good luck with this!

Chapter 6

TIME MANAGEMENT PRINCIPALS: PRIORITIES, FOCUS & ENERGY

Now let's discuss the single thing that most clearly and truly defines success for business more than anything else I've encountered: *how you, the business owner, spend your time.* That's our focus here.

I've seen many businesses with great strategies, good tactics, and strong execution. But the number one thing that limits them is *how the business owner spends their time.* Why? *Because time is the one resource that is irrecoverable.* Once it's gone, *it's gone.* You can't get it back. So your #1 priority as a business owner must be *ensuring you are spending your time as wisely as possible.*

Furthermore, since you're the owner, everyone on your team watches how you're using your time. You set the example for all of your employees. Because of this, I want to discuss some specific tactics for (1) getting better at knowing how to most effectively use your time, and (2) ensuring you're spending it on things that matter the most to your life and business.

PRIORITIES, FOCUS, AND ENERGY

This is an area where you'll have to make small, incremental changes. There's simply no way to make all these changes at once. This is a step-by-step process.

This is important because spending your time on the right activities *must become a habit for you!* You may not realize this, but all of your behaviors right now, particularly with the way you use your time throughout the day, are already habits. So you've got to change your bad habits, which takes time. You simply can't form radically different habits overnight. Instead, you need to make small changes over time.

So let's cover three specific areas to work on to shift the habits that dictate your ability to manage your time well: **Priorities**, **Focus** and **Energy**.

You're going to have to try a few things before you find the strategies that work best for you, but I want to start you off with some ideas I know are strong to get the ball rolling.

PRIORITIES

The first area is *priorities.* Without priorities, everything appears urgent. We can get into an "I'll work on that when I get to it" mode. But if we don't see it or if it doesn't come to us, what happens then? This ends up being a "squeaky wheel" approach many business owners find themselves trapped in with no room for priorities.

Let me illustrate an approach to avoid this by sharing a story of one of my best mentors, a CEO of a billion-dollar company. He ran a fairly complicated business with 11 direct reports. Because we were big, you might think that the CEO was pulled in multiple directions. But this was not the case. In fact, I was amazed by how well he handled his difficult role.

Here's what he did:

1. For each of the 11 members of his leadership team, he identified three specific strategies he wanted them to focus on. He thought deeply about where he wanted the business to go and boiled that down into three priorities for each of us.

2. Next, he prepared a single sheet of paper for each of his direct reports with the three priorities listed on it, and once a week, he would hold a one-on-one meeting with each of us. These meetings were pre-scheduled and largely non-negotiable. That meant he had 11 one-on-one meetings

every week. At each meeting he'd pull our individual sheet out of his desk drawer and lay it on his desk. It was the *only thing* on his desk—our sheet of paper with our three priorities written on it.

3. Meetings went like this: he'd ask about the first priority and we'd update him. He'd ask a few questions and always end by saying, "What help do you need from me?" The right answer was, "I got it. I don't need any help." Because otherwise, he'd jump in and help. Then he'd move to the second priority and we'd repeat the same process, every week.

4. Once we were done with his top three priorities, if there was any time left, we could bring up anything that was on our list, but only *after* the priorities he had set. He consistently repeated this with each of his eleven direct reports.

That's it! He spent essentially 11 hours a week focused on three specific things for 11 of us. That meant 33 major priorities were getting done in the business without him having to do one bit of work and he still had most of his week left! Now, how about that?

Find Your Strategy

What about you? Do you have a team of 3–4 that you might be able to give a few priorities to each? Can you find some way to focus on these each week?

 TUNE-UP TIP: Having trouble prioritizing? Try reading a book. There are tons of helpful books on the subject, like *Eat That Frog*. It's an easy read that really illustrates why you should do the most important things first. Once they are out of the way, everything else is downhill. Find a way to focus on priorities like this that works for you. So go find a book or two on the topic.

FOCUS

Now let's talk about *focus*. We need to assess how you currently focus your time when you need to get something done. What strategy do you use to focus on just one thing? Do you even have one? If your strategy is *multitasking*, let's stop and look at that for a moment.

I hear people talk all the time about multitasking like they are proud of themselves. Do you claim to be a great multitasker? Reality check folks, *no one* is great at "multitasking." All you're really doing is *switching focus from one thing to another and back again.* And as a result, it's impossible to be as efficient as when you are focused deeply on a single activity.

So how do you focus? Here are a couple of strategies to get you started:

- **Strategy #1:** Work in 30–40-minute "sprint" periods. Pick something that's a priority, set aside 30–40 minutes, and do whatever it takes to get to a quiet place where you *know* you can focus *without interruption.* I *guarantee* you'll get *far more* done in that 30–40 minutes than you would just working intermittently on the same issue throughout the day or week. What's different? *Focus.* That's the vital ingredient.

- **Strategy #2:** The world is *filled* with distractions. In fact, you probably have a device or app that's dinging you right now. There are *always* things happening. If you're reading this in an e-reader, you may even have your email open on another part of your screen. So what's the strategy? **Turn off what distracts you!** Whatever it is, *simply turn it off!*

Remember, your business is a reflection of you. You, the business owner, must demonstrate wise use of your time. You *must* be willing to ignore that text message or email alert until certain times during the day. I know that this is hard, but focus on making small, incremental changes that build new habits. Distractions are a time suck. You and I both know it, so let's do something about it!

TUNE-UP TIP: Someone gave me this brilliant idea: when somebody distracts you, they want one of three things: (1) to schedule time with you, (2) to get some information from you or, (3) to engage you in a project of some kind (give you work). Here's a simple approach to use: whenever somebody comes in and interrupts you, *before* listening to what they need, first tell them what *you're working on.*

They might say, "Hey, Rich! Got a minute?" To which I'd say, "Sure. But I'm working on this video series right now, what have you got?" In other words, tell them politely, but directly, *"Hey, here's what I'm working on right now."* This way they know you don't have much time so they need to be brief. **Be up front and tell people who interrupt what you're working on. They'll respond to the fact you're busy and quickly let you get back to your priority work.**

ENERGY

Besides priority and focus, your *energy* is the third critical ingredient. It's the lifeblood you need to function. Without it, you feel drained. However, everyone has a slightly different daily biological energy clock. For me, there are some times when I'm just more fired up than others. I'm a morning person. My biological clock is geared to get me up and going early.

But then in the afternoon I tend to fade. I have to think about how and when I consume food or my energy flat lines. I also have to get up and get my blood flowing to maintain energy. What about you? When is your "power time" of the day? *Reserve that time for your most important tasks!* Are you aware of low energy times? How can you keep your energy high during those down periods?

If you follow the sprint model, during your down time you can take a walk. Get outside, do a few jumping jacks, have a healthy snack, or do whatever it is you need to manage your energy for your next sprint session.

The goal here is to help you manage your time better, so think of one or two small changes you'd like to make. Maybe you manage your cool downs between sprint sessions better or find a quieter place to focus? Maybe you start limiting interruptions by telling people what you are doing before listening to them? Whatever it is, create new habits by changing your behaviors and actions.

Remember, as the business owner, you set the standard for everyone in your business. If employees see you always distracted by your smart phone (your "weapon of mass distraction"), they'll assume they can do the same thing. If a customer walks in and you check your phone rather than focusing on them, your team will do the same because your behavior teaches them what is acceptable in your business. You *MUST* set proper time management standards or you sabotage your own efforts.

 TUNE-UP TIP: Pick out one or two changes suggested in this chapter that you believe you can implement immediately and put them into practice right away. By setting a new example of time management built on **priorities, focus,** and **energy**, you can not only become more productive, but also help your people get more done in their day as well.

Chapter 7
LIFE BALANCE

So just what is *life balance?* Think of it this way: we typically only realize we need balance when we're *out of balance*. Think back to the first time you got on a bike. My dad had to hold the seat and run along behind me while I tried to learn how to create balance by (1) *recognizing when I was out of balance,* and (2) *making corrections to try to regain my balance.*

So first is recognizing if you are out of balance, which is *not easy to do*. That's why so many business owners are so maniacally focused on business that *they're totally unaware of other areas of their life!* Good news though, I have an exercise designed to help with this.

THE FOUR CIRCLE EXERCISE

Think of someone whose life was so out of balance they were completely unaware of things in some areas. We've all known people like this. They fall into the trap of thinking that focusing solely on their job is good for their family and don't even notice what's going on with them. But it is critical to balance work with other parts of your life or you'll have no life at all.

Please don't make the same mistake my father made in thinking that work is all there is to your life. Your business is *only* a tool, nothing more. Remember that. This exercise will help you recognize and get tuned-in to whether or not you are out of balance.

Setting Up Your Four Circles

Start by getting some paper or your notebook.

Step One: Draw four circles in the four quadrants of the paper much like the four in the image above.

Step Two: Label each circle as follows (again, following the image above):

- **Home:** Families take up a lot of time, so they need their own circle.
- **Work:** Like family, work demands enough time to need its own circle.
- **Community:** This circle is for anything that demands your time because of your role in your community. The more successful your business becomes, the more demands you will have in this circle.
- **Self:** No true balance is attained without a little me-time. This is when you dream, enjoy, go to nature, read, workout, or whatever *you* need. If

you don't have this circle, you'll never have the reserves to handle the other three.

These are the four major areas you need to balance in your life. As you are probably aware, this requires a thoughtful plan to be successful.

The Right Way To Balance Your Four Circles

So the first major issue is finding time for all four circles. That is, finding time for work and then still having time to be a good spouse, parent, and friend. You might worry thinking, *how will I have any me-time, energy or find time to help random people in the community? You're kidding, right?* Don't panic, I have a plan!

I want you to think about ways you can achieve "multiple wins." Instead of trying to hit a single, hit a double, triple, or home run. Look for ways where something that you're doing for work *could also benefit another circle, like community.*

Start with yourself—is there some way you could accomplish your *Me Time* while also positively impacting your family, business, or community? In other words, *look at what you are doing for ways to combine activities to maximize your efforts across multiple circles of your life!*

Examples Of Ways To Combine Different Circles

Here are some examples of how to combine these circles:

- A client recently moved in to a new office space where in each office he placed a piece of workout equipment. A treadmill in one office, a Stairmaster in another, and so on. Equipment is in every office, and he installed showers in the bathrooms. Now his *entire team* can work *and* stay fit—*providing better life balance for everyone in his business!* If balancing your life helps your business, how much more does balancing *everyone's* life help your business?
- Got a favorite charity in the community? Involve your family in it. Now you're taking care of your family and community making more room for that precious *me time* and increasing *life balance!*

- Take that last idea one step further: what if you brought the charity into your office and engaged your staff with it as a weekend project or team activity? You've heard of fun runs and other fundraising activity. Doing something like this would allow you to combine community, family, and work all at once.

See how it works? This is *not* about partitioning your life into the four quadrants. No, lives just can't be divided up like that. So don't think about these areas as separate from one another. Instead, think about combining them for multiple wins. All it takes is a little purposeful pre-thought.

Looking Ahead With Your Four Circles

This exercise can be extremely helpful in balancing your life with the right approach. Here are some tips to help achieve that approach:

1. First, forget the notion that life balance means spending 4 hours here, 4 hours there, and so on. Don't try that because you'll never make it. The math won't work.
2. Instead, look for ways to leverage and combine your circles like *bring your daughter or son to work, involve your work in your community service activity, etc.* Your priority is to find effective ways to do this instead of tracking how much time you spend where.

THE FOUR COLORS

I have one more valuable resource I want to share with you that a colleague of mine created. It's a website *www.NoBrownDays.com*. It has some great resources & tools to help you build an ideal schedule for your life. It helps you focus your schedule on four primary areas:

1. Revenue generating or **green** activities (the color of money);
2. Administrative or **red** activities (think *red tape*);
3. Strategy & think-time or **blue** activities (like a blue sky); and
4. Rest & relaxation time or **yellow** activities (mellow-yellow time).

The idea is that ideally *you focus on a single color each day*. You schedule out your calendar in a way that every day has a primary focus designated by one of these four colors. I love his concept and have been applying it to my business because it's fantastic at helping me with energy generation and focus.

As busy business owners, that's not how we tend to schedule our days. We tend to mix all these different activities. But instead of a colorful rainbow leading to a pot of gold, all we get is crap-stain brown color every day for weeks, months, or even years!

So www.NoBrownDays.com is a conceptual tool set to help you get some real power, focus, and balance in your life. I recommend you check it out.

With each concept or exercise we go over, I want you to *make it work for you*. I've given you several different ideas not because I expect you to do everything. I do, however, expect you to start with these ideas and *keep trying things until you find ones that work for you.*

Chapter 8
YOUR TEAM OF ADVISORS

Y our team of advisors are the people you surround yourself with and rely on, your go-to folks. These are people you can call on anytime to help you with any business challenge. Have you identified such a team already? Maybe you call them by a different name and call them often. If so, great!

If you don't have such a team, you need one. Every business owner must face the truth that **no one individual is smart enough run a business on their own.** Often I hear business owners say, "What could you help with? I've been running this business for 25 years." Sadly, the reality for many of them is they don't have 25 years of experience, they have one year of business experience repeated 25 times. They've been doing things the same since day one and largely by themselves. Nobody can create a significant and sustainable business by themselves. *It just can't happen.*

TOP PROFESSIONALS ALWAYS HAVE A TEAM OF ADVISORS

Consider those at the top of their game, like superstar sports athletes. They typically have two or three advisors like a head coach, a positions coach, a weight training coach, and so on. In baseball there are 3rd and 1st base coaches watching each play from a different position. Sure a player may step up to the plate by themselves, but their team of advisors is there keeping an eye out for what they cannot see. If you want this kind of success, you need the same kind of assistance—no matter who you are. I know I need it, we *all* do.

THE STAR EXERCISE

Spend some time right now thinking about your team of advisors. If you don't know where to begin, don't worry. Get your journal again. This time, draw a big 5-pointed star like this one:

In the middle of the star is YOU, the business owner. Each point of the star is a different aspect of your business where you'll need an advisor on your team.

The Five Points On Your Star = The Five Responsibilities Of The Business Owner

As your business develops, there are five specific things (see above image) you, as the business owner, are responsible for:

1. **Creating Value:** You're in the business of *creating value*. You've got a responsibility to *create value* for your business in the marketplace.

2. **Compounding Value:** You must also *compound your business's value*. Take the value that you create to the next level and multiply it. For example, make your business larger to incrementally (or better yet exponentially) grow the value you've created.

3. **Protecting Value:** Once you've developed, grown, and compounded a valuable business, you must *protect that value*.

4. **Distributing Value:** Eventually you'll need to *distribute the value you've helped create*. Shareholders or other investors in your business want and expect a return on their investment.

5. **Transferring Value:** Ultimately, you're going to *transfer value* to someone else, whether that is to your kids, your employees through an employee stock ownership program, or by selling your business on the market.

Think about your job as the business owner in terms of needing to do these five things. I'm not smart enough to do all these things by myself. I simply don't have all the tools or knowledge I'd need. I may know my business, but I can't do everything on this star chart efficiently enough for my business. I need help. I need a *team of advisors*.

Different Advisors For Different Areas

You will need some *topic-specific* advisors. For example, here are some of the advisors you may want on your team:

- **A Business Banker** you can trust. You need to develop a relationship with a solid one.

- **A CPA** that knows your business well, understands your issues, and can advise you on accounting and tax issues.
- **A Financial Planner** who can help you grow, share, invest, and protect the wealth you create with your business.
- **A Business Coach/Advisor** who knows the value of your business and can help make it even more profitable with specific business-building strategies.
- **An HR/Benefits Consultant** who can help you understand and navigate legal changes and advise you regarding your team's programs and coverages.
- **A Business Broker** who can help you position your business for maximum market value as you draw closer to your transition date.
- **A Business Insurance Consultant** to assist in making certain your business is well covered from liability and unexpected disasters.

Spend some time on your list. Who do you have in these roles today? Write their first names down on the star because *you must be on the first name basis with each of your advisors.*

THREE CRITERIA TO USE WHEN FILLING AN EMPTY SPOT ON YOUR STAR

If you have an open spot on your star, talk to your colleagues and engage with professionally-minded folks you know and ask, "Who do you work with or know in this area that could be a resource to me and my business?"

Then, pick 2–3 potential advisors and interview them. As you do, don't expect to find the right advisor on your first or second meeting. It's important to find an advisor that both understands *and* is interested in your business. Consider these three criteria when interviewing an advisor:

1. If you call them, ***will they pick up and answer?*** If they're not going to answer your phone call when you need immediate insight or advice, then they probably shouldn't be on your star.

2. If they do take your call, ***would you get a bill as a result?*** If you think it's impossible to find an attorney you can call without getting billed, that's simply not true. If you look, you can find consultants or attorneys that don't bill if you just pick up the phone to check-in, get an update, or ask a quick question.

3. ***Do they know your business well enough to help you make critical business decisions?*** Lastly, consider how well those on your list know your specific business. You want advisors with insider knowledge of your business. You want them to know your business well enough to understand where you're going and what your long term goals are.

Make sure that you have people *in each one of these roles that you can rely on* before you move forward. Make sure that they both *get you* and *have your best interests in mind.*

SECTION TWO

THE HANDLE BARS
OF YOUR BUSINESS

Chapter 9

LEARNING TO STEER
YOUR BUSINESS

To get people to follow you, you must be inspiring, which requires leadership and vision. Think about the behaviors of someone you admire. Anyone with a following has a vision for what they want to accomplish. You see, vision *is what motivates people to move forward.* My dad had a vision, and while it may seem small in hindsight, at the time it seemed huge and unattainable. Even now I can remember discussing it like it was yesterday:

We were at the kitchen table following a long Saturday of work. Dad was following his routine of recording the day's transactions in his Big Chief tablet. He counted both total houses completed and cash generated. This particular day had been *very* good and we knew it. The big question was, *had it been our BEST ever?*

We started early that morning in a suburb where all the homes were similarly laid out: two stories with 7–8 windows downstairs and 4 more upstairs—the perfect setup for a 3-man crew. One guy with the big ladder on the upstairs windows, another on the downstairs windows, and the third to wash the windows on the front and back doors as well as talk briefly to the homeowner and present the $7.00 bill.

We spent the entire day in that suburb, stopping only for a quick lunch and working until well after 6:00 pm. When it was over, we were exhausted but proud. My older brother and I were anxiously waiting to hear the tally. We wanted to know if we'd set a new single day record in houses completed and money collected.

After double-checking, Dad proudly declared "We knocked out over 60 houses today!" We had done it! We had washed the windows of more than 60 houses in a single day, a feat never before accomplished by Allen & Sons Window Washing! With a $7.00 average fee for each house, our receipts for the day were over $400! We were the new world record holders!

It was right then that Dad proudly stood up and declared his new vision for our future. Riding high, Dad predicted that we would "own" Lindhurst—the suburb we'd worked in. "One day we will do the windows on every home in the Lindhurst neighborhood!" That was my dad's vision of the future.

Lindhurst had *hundreds*, maybe even *thousands* of homes where we were working. So we did some quick math and figured out it would take us around 30 days to make it to each home. This seemed perfect since we would typically wash each home's windows once a month—we could just start anew each month. We could work that one neighborhood and never have to go anywhere else. Every day would be 60+ houses and a $400 payday. We were on top of the world (at least our world)!

That's how *inspiring* my dad's vision was. And we were excited to help him make it happen. The possibilities that lie ahead dazzled us. And in that moment, it worked. We were all along with him for the ride.

This is what vision can do for your business. This is the reaction you want from your team when you share with them your vision.

Chapter 10

PURPOSE

When it comes to your role as the business owner, providing *Leadership & Vision* are #1 on the list. They are your most critical assignment. This is important for you, your team, and your customers. You need to do everything you can to be as *clear, concise, and specific as possible* about where you're taking your business and what you want your business to become.

Owning a business is a journey. Your business is moving forward down the road. Remember, **your hands are on the handlebars—you're the one steering!** So let's make sure you steer with a purpose.

STEERING WITH PURPOSE

This is an incredible responsibility but also very exciting. This is where you as a business owner can truly set yourself apart because many business owners *just don't give this much thought.* They're focused on the *details* of the business. Instead, I want you focused on *vision, leadership, and where you're taking your business.*

What is your purpose? Why do you own your business? What drives you? Sure, you may have started it out of practicality. I get that. But, if you really want your business to reach its potential, you need to be crystal clear about *your* purpose. To help, I want to suggest some resources because this topic is far too important for a single chapter.

This is one of those areas where you can find much greater depth elsewhere. Several individuals have done far more work on this topic. Some even inspired this book, like the ones I want to tell you about here.

DRIVE BY DANIEL PINK

One inspiration for this book is Daniel Pink's book *Drive*. I strongly recommend you read this book. In the meantime, you can get a quick synopsis by searching YouTube for "*Drive* by Daniel Pink." There's a 20-minute overview video that demonstrates how *purpose* is one of the three most compelling motivators for people.

Purpose makes people—both those who work for and those who do business with you—motivated to choose you over the guy down the street. *Drive* is a "must-read" for any business owner.

START WITH WHY BY SIMON SINEK

Another business author who I find genuinely inspiring is Simon Sinek, author of a book titled *Start with Why*. I highly encourage you read it. Simon has done *tremendous* work determining why starting with *why* is essential to your business's purpose. Like *Drive,* you'll find a YouTube video that helps explain concepts in his book.

Basically, Simon's concept is that there are three different ways to describe your business:

1. **The *What* of your Business:** This is *what* you do: serve fried chicken, fix computers, or sell used automobiles. This is the *what*, the answer you give when someone asks, "So what is it you do?"
2. **The *How* of your Business:** Next is the *how*, what typically differentiates one business from another. For example, two realtors may both sell real estate, but *how* they do it is where they are different.
3. **The What of your Business:** At the center of everything is the *why* of your business. Most business owners describe their business like, "Here's **what** I do, and here's **how** I do it." Most haven't given much thought to

the why or structured their business thinking around, "Here's why this is so important to me."

The problem with describing your business in this order is that this is a fairly typical and un-compelling sales pitch. What Sinek suggests is *we go from the inside-out*. In other words, **we start with the *why*, then explain the *how* and lastly, the *what*.**

The Neocortex Vs. The Limbic System

Starting with the *why* is important because the *what* typically gets processed by the logic center in our brain, the neocortex. This part of the brain handles analysis and details. By starting with *what*, you invite people to process the information with their neocortex, the logic center of the brain.

In contrast, the *why* is processed by the limbic system, the part of the brain that controls emotions. Your message can be more impactful when processed by the emotion center rather than the logical center. Research supports the notion that consumer buying decisions are 80% based on emotion and only 20% based on logic.

Just look at your own big purchases. What *truly* motivated them? Sure, it may have been a good buy, but is that *why* you bought it? Isn't it rather that you felt it in your gut on some intangible level? This *means you were processing the decision through your limbic system.*

  TUNE-UP TIP: When you talk or think about your business, put the focus first and foremost on the *purpose* of your business, the *why*. The emotional core behind your business that will help you engage prospects' limbic system instead of their neocortex. Once they get the *why*, anyone can get behind the *what*. So it's getting people to understand the *why*, not the *what,* of your business that will truly set you apart.

LEARNING TO TELL AND SHARE YOUR STORY

After reading the books recommended above, take some time to craft your own story. Articulate your own version of why you are a business owner.

You may be worried that you don't have a compelling story or that there's not much to it. I promise you, *this just isn't true.* Start digging into how you got into your industry, what compelled you to start your business. Before long, genuine elements of a truly emotional story will begin to emerge.

We all have a story. Just think of this book. Think of how I started with the *why.* Think of how I start each section with a new story about my dad. You know my dad is what brought me to this place, that he is what compels me to take this journey with you. There are a lot of people who do *what* I do, and there are a lot of people who do *what* you do. BUT, each of us has a different *why.* My *why* drives me to do something unique, so does your *why.* You *do* have a story to tell, and I want you to learn to tell it.

Practice Telling Your Story

We all have smart phones these days. So take out yours and simply record yourself for five minutes telling your story. Just share it right from your heart. Be personal and genuine.

Imagine you're leaving your child or grandchild a story about you for when they're older. Give colorful details. Answer questions like: Where were you? What did you struggle with? Why was this important? Tell *your* story. Share it with someone, a confidant or spouse who will give good feedback. The more you practice, the better you will become at telling your story in a genuine way.

Eventually, share your story with your team members. They'll be even more motivated to work with you once they see and understand the path you've taken to get to where you're at with your business.

The goal is to get to the point where you can share your story with everyone—including your customers. Just like with your team, your story will motivate customers to follow you. And those who don't follow? *That's fine.* They're not your ideal customer. But those who relate to your story will be far more loyal in the future. Take some time with this, I know it will be hard at first, but it's a great way to bring many great things to your business.

LEARN WHAT DRIVES YOU

I have one last exercise to help you do some deep thinking about what drives you. Ask yourself questions like:

- What's something in the world around you that you care about?
- What's something in your community or country you're really impassioned by?
- What's something you're so tired of that you want to do something about it?

Make this thing *the purpose of your business*. Make it what benefits from your business's success and then go help solve or cure the issue you have chosen. Everybody's got one. For example:

- Maybe someone you know has died from cancer or another disease you can fight?
- Maybe child hunger is particularly heavy on your heart?
- Maybe your hometown has a homelessness problem you'd like to help with?
- Maybe you are a veteran and want to help other veterans or active military personal?

Whatever the purpose is, relate it to your business. People like supporting a cause other than simply making a business owner wealthy. This isn't about putting money in your wallet. Maybe that is a by-product, but the real purpose is so that you can make an impact on the world through your business—not just make money. We all have a different purpose. Figure out what yours is.

Before moving on, make sure that you:

- Really understand your purpose
- Can tell your story in a clear and compelling manner
- Know the cause you want to support
- Have all of these things baked into every aspect of your business

This is what's going to compel people. Motivate yourself, then your team, your customers, and all of your business relationships. I promise you—*this is powerful stuff!*

Chapter 11

VISION

You've heard the saying "If you don't know where you're going, then any road will get you there." Well the same is true with your business. If you don't know where you're heading, then how do you know what direction to steer?

Purpose is *why* you steer and vision is *where* you steer. And just like steering a bike, if you don't pay attention, you'll find yourself driving into a ditch. This is *very important for a business owner,* an area where you **must** spend a significant amount of your time.

KNOWING WHERE YOU ARE GOING

If you don't have a good idea where you want your business to be ten years from now, how will have any chance of getting there? You might be thinking, *Rich, I don't even know what my business will be like six months from now! How could I possibly know what it should look like in 10 years?* I hear that. But hear this: **you must visualize where you are headed if you truly want to get there.**

You don't just hop on a bike and randomly end up at your cousin's house 25 miles away. *Nope.* No businesses accidentally become a Fortune 500 company either. Want to grow? *Then you need a vision of what that growth should look like.*

Doing so activates a part of our brain called the *Reticular Activating System (RAS)* that helps tune into the things around you. Here's a story to illustrate this:

When my son turned 16, he came to me and informed me that he didn't want just any car for his first one. He wanted a '69 Mustang. I told him that sounded great and asked him to find a picture of the car he hoped to someday own. He found one and put it on the mirror in his bedroom. Beneath it, I placed a large jar and told him, "You collect your money here, I'll match you, and we'll go find you a '69 Mustang."

Over the next several months he put money into the jar. This went on until one weekend while driving back through Oklahoma from visiting the grandparents, my son yells out, "Hey Dad! Look!" I looked to my left and sure enough, there's a '69 Mustang on the side of the road with a big *FOR SALE* sign on it.

We made a U-turn and came back to check out the car. We called the phone number on the window, and the owner agreed to come open up the car. We fired up the car, took it for a short drive, and without even getting it inspected, we bought it—never stopping to question if we might find a Mustang in better condition or at a better price. We made the purchase on an *emotional* impulse.

Guess what happened next? *No matter where my son took that car, he'd run into other old Mustangs.* Turns out they were everywhere and always had been. We'd just never noticed them because we weren't tuned in, because *we hadn't set our RAS.*

You have to *set your RAS,* or *have a vision,* to see the things around you—*even the things right in front of your face.* Once you are tuned in, you'll start to see things that relate to it—just like my son and his Mustang.

THE MOUNTAIN TOP EXERCISE

Imagine for a minute you're on a path with your bike that leads to a location at the top of a mountain. This location represents where your business will be in ten years. Getting an image here? Sketch it out if that helps.

The path you take up any mountain will never be a straight line. As you grow and expand over the next 10 years, there'll be some bumps, valleys, climbs, and maybe even a few unforeseen detours. However, as long as you stay the path, *you will* get to that mountain top.

To do that, you need to know where you are starting from, that is where your business is today as well as where you'll be in 10 years. So you need to write down both where you are and where you ultimately want to be.

Start with the mountaintop. Describe what it looks like. Include details like:

- How many team members do you have?
- What locations do you have?
- What products or services do you offer?
- How are you organized?
- Who is your ideal customer?
- What is your volume?
- How is your business structured?
- What is your daily life like?
- How involved with the business are you?
- Do you still run the business? If not, what are you doing?
- How do you spend your time?

There is no right or wrong answer here. What's important is that these details accurately represent where you want to go. Define the view in clear detail—the clearer, the better. Don't worry about whether it will actually turn out this way. Focus instead on learning to think about your business in terms of where you are headed not just where you are now.

From 10 To 1 In Four Steps

Let's flip the script. Instead of starting with a one-year plan and trying to work out to ten years, start at year ten and work backwards to determine your one-year plan. Here are four simple steps to help you do just that:

- **STEP ONE:** Describe what your business will be like in 10 years. Be specific and think in colorful detail. Ask yourself, *what do I truly want this business to look like when I reach the mountain top?*
- **STEP TWO:** Once you have the 10-year vision down in writing, then step back to 5 years away and ask, *where do I need to be in five years to*

make sure I'm on track to hit the 10-year point? Again, write this down in detail.

- **STEP THREE:** With the 5-year vision clearly defined, bring your thinking back to just three years from now. Once again, ask yourself, *where do I need to be in three years to be on track to reach my 5-year vision?*
- **STEP FOUR:** With the 3-year vision clearly defined, bring your thinking back to just one year in the future. Ask the same question, *where do I need to be next year to be on track to reach my 3-year vision?*

Now you have a very specific outline of your one year, three year, five year, AND ten year vision! See how following these steps can start a plan and structure for your business? Now you can tell if you are on pace to make what you need to make happen, and if not, you have a good idea of what needs to be modified or adjusted.

This is far better than just letting your business happen. Don't just go on about your daily activities and hope you'll one day end up where you want to be. Instead, plan out where you want to be and use a vision to guide you.

THE VISION-BOARD EXERCISE

For this exercise, I want you to involve your significant other if you have one. You can do it on your own if you prefer, but it's best to get them involved if possible. You'll be creating what I call a *Vision Board*. Here's how it works:

- **STEP ONE:** Get yourself a large sheet of construction paper similar to what an elementary school student might use for an art project.
- **STEP TWO:** Get a stack of old magazines—any will do. Also grab a pair of scissors, a glue stick, and some markers.
- **STEP THREE:** Sit down with your significant other and cut out all the pictures, words, phrases, images, etc., that describe what you want your life to be like in the future. Just start tearing, cutting, and gluing them onto your construction paper to make a collage (this makes for a great date-night).

- **ALTERNATE STEP THREE:** You and your spouse each make your own collage. It will be fun and interesting to share your board with your life-long partner. Do what works for you. I've seen it work both ways. Both are compelling.
- **STEP FOUR:** When your collage is finished, step back and look at it. You might be surprised at how it inspires you or what you learn about your spouse's vision board. Who knows? You might spark a genuine and healthy conversation about where you are headed like you've never had before.

This is a *VISION* Board, so it works best with pictures, image, and phrases that inspire you. It will be extremely helpful at times when things get rough, when you hit a bump or a snag.

At those critical times, you need motivation. Motivation you can find *by looking at your Vision Board!* When you are down, you can look at it and remember why you are working so hard. I promise you, this *will* motivate you and *will* drive you to create the future you envision.

 TUNE-UP TIP: Looking for a little more balance? Call your Vision Board Exercise, "Date Night," and suddenly you're hitting two of your circles at once and maximizing your efforts! This is a great way to combine your business needs with your need to carve out a bit more time to be more intimate with your spouse!

THE PERFECT DAY EXERCISE

One final, short assignment—take out a piece of paper and write on it what your perfect day looks like. Include details like:

- When would you wake up?
- What would you eat?
- Where would you be?
- Who would you be with?
- What type of activities would you do?
- How would you close that day?

The point here is *to get inside your own head,* because once you know what your perfect day looks like, your RAS will be set and you can start to make it come to life one step at a time.

The whole purpose of vision is knowing where we want to be in the future, so we know if we're making progress towards our goals. So whether your goal is a perfect day or something on your vision board, you know where you want to be—*vision* is essential.

Chapter 12

PERFORMANCE STANDARDS

Why are Performance Standards so important? Well, if your intention is to do things just like everyone else, why even bother owning a business? If you're not going to put out a better product than your competitor, why put out any effort at all?

You must *set your business apart*. One of the best ways to do this is by setting performance standards that *create uniqueness*. Setting standards higher than your strongest competition prevents your business from having to compete on the basis of price. Trust me, almost anything would be better than running a business that only has price as its competitive differentiation.

Setting performance standards allows you to *steer* your business away from this type of business model. The goal is to define your performance standard with a *one-word* or *one-phrase description*. Start by thinking of a word that defines the standards you are going to set for your company. Let me give you an example to follow.

HIGH POINT UNIVERSITY

My youngest daughter recently made her decision on which college to attend. Back in high school, she was actively searching for the "perfect" college. Over her spring break junior year, we took a trip to visit some schools in the southeast—Tennessee, North Carolina, Duke, Georgia, and Auburn. The programs and traditions on display during the trip were impressive and exciting. But among these large, well-known universities, we decided to visit a smaller school named *High Point University.*

High Point came to my attention through an interview in *Success Magazine* with the university's president, Dr. Nido Qubein. In the interview, he claimed that over the past 10 years, he had helped convert High Point University from a no-name college into one of the most prestigious in the southeast. As I listened to Dr. Qubein describe High Point University, the high performance standard he set at the university was clear, a standard he called *"Extraordinary."*

He used a single, powerful word, *extraordinary,* to define High Point University. So we decided to see if Dr. Qubein's claims about High Point University were true. *What did we find?* Just like he said, everything on campus and about the school was remarkably *extraordinary!*

My daughter, her mother, and I had already experienced several of the larger universities so we thought we knew what to expect when we arrived. We had typically found a visitor parking lot and signs directing us "To Admissions Office" where we'd be given a visitor's packet.

High Point, however, was different from the moment we hit campus. The parking lot specifically designated for prospective students was attended by its own security guard. He came up to our car and spoke to my daughter directly. Once he learned her name, he immediately responded with, "Anne Drew, we've been waiting for you! Your parking spot is right this way!"

He pointed to one of twenty parking spots with a lit LED sign that reading "High Point University Welcomes..." Our spot read, "Anne Drew Allen from Texas." The officer let us know that this was our spot for the day. Come or go as we please, it was ours to use. He also gave her the packet we normally had to go hunting for and wished us an enjoyable visit.

Extraordinary.

The classroom buildings were, believe it or not, *extraordinary.* They were modeled after Fortune 500 corporate headquarters, very upscale. In fact, as you walked in and out of different buildings on campus, you were greeted with classical music playing on speakers hidden in the large, welcoming trees.

Everywhere there was an *extraordinary* sense of inspiration. Bronze statues of great people from the past that we are inspired by and aspire to, like Aristotle and Madame Curie, sat on benches across campus.

Extraordinary.

This was just a 4000-person school, but with three cafeterias on campus: a standard campus cafeteria, a second, all-organic health food cafeteria, and a third, five-star fine-dining restaurant located on the top floor of the newest building on campus. Each week students could dine there as part of their regular meal plan. Reservations were required in advance and on each visit, students were given etiquette tips. They could even bring a guest for $50, but under no circumstances could they use their cell phones. This was expressly forbidden, which required them to enjoy a formal evening of fine dining and finer conversation!

Extraordinary.

Everything was extraordinary and had to be in order to compete with the other schools in the region like Wake Forest and Duke. They had to define who they were to stand out, so they chose to define their university as *extraordinary*.

Can you see why setting a performance standard is so important? Could you envision what your business would be like if you had a single word or single-phrase performance standard that defined who you were as a business?

So I ask you, *what are your performance standards?* What standards will you hold your team accountable to? What will you do so your customers can *see, feel,* and *sense* how your business stands out the way High Point University does?

Now *extraordinary* may not be right for you. It might be too big. Fair enough, but let me give you some other examples to show you what you *can* do that you might not realize.

RESORT-QUALITY POOL CLEANING SERVICES

Here's another example. I work with a pool cleaning company. After a brainstorming session, it was decided to set the performance standard as **Resort-Quality Service.** Think about that for a moment. *What do you imagine when* *think of a pool at a resort?* Everything is clean, people are in uniform, and the grounds are spotless. This phrase worked for this business. Employees knew *exactly* how to dress and how to behave. It didn't take long for the team to catch on and clients to take notice.

They wear resort-style uniforms and greet all customers with a polite "ma'am" or "sir" just like at a resort. They arrange anything out of place as well so the pool area is clean and neat to ensure customers have a *resort-quality* experience in their own backyard. This standard completely *transformed* the way team members saw themselves. Customers noticed the superior service standards, and responded.

SERVICE AND BEYOND...

I have another client that provides municipality fleet services. They maintain and care for company vehicles like sedans, light duty trucks, police cruisers, and fire trucks. This client decided on the performance standard, *"Service and Beyond."* This became their "catch-phrase." On a regular basis, my client would ask each team member, "What are you doing to provide Service and Beyond?"

As a result, his Fleet Department decided that each time they serviced a vehicle for any reason, *before giving it back that they'd wash and refuel it!* Now, every customer who picks up their vehicle finds it was not only serviced, but cleaned and refueled. Now that's *Service and Beyond* that customers stand up and notice. Hopefully this helps you see that no matter what your business is, there is a performance standard that will help you *steer* ahead of your competition with consistently superior products or service.

Think about your most difficult competition and ask, *what could you do to set yourself apart from them?* What standard could you set so that everybody in your target audience could see your service or products are superior to this competitor where it matters most? Standards help you steer *ahead of the competition.* That's why you need *vision.* Performance standards tell your team what you expect from them and your customers what to expect from you.

Your business can no longer be "everybody do it the way you want." No, you're in business for specific reasons guided by specific performance standards.

So before you move on, ask yourself: *What do I want and CHOOSE to be?* This is a big decision for you and your business.

Remember, this is **YOUR** standard, so hold firm to it once you set it. If you don't, no one else will either.

Chapter 13

YOUR STRATEGIC SUMMARY

I want to give you a framework to document and effectively communicate your new leadership strategy to the rest of you team. We'll do this by creating a document called a *strategic summary*: a **strategic** way to **summarize** your thoughts together into a concise two-page document that accurately describes how your business works. An example of a strategic summary is on the next page.

Now the document you create may need to be quite a bit different from this one, that's ok. But using a summary like this is a powerful tool I've seen work time and time again. As you can tell, there's too much here to go over in detail in a single chapter. But we'll return to this summary at later points in the book. Keep your eyes out for blueprints for your summary throughout the remainder of the book. Having the framework now should help you put your summary together and fill in the blanks when you come to the appropriate sections.

To begin, your strategic summary needs to include your purpose, vision, and performance standards as we've covered in this section:

- **Purpose (Why):** Answer questions like, *why are you in business? What are you about?*

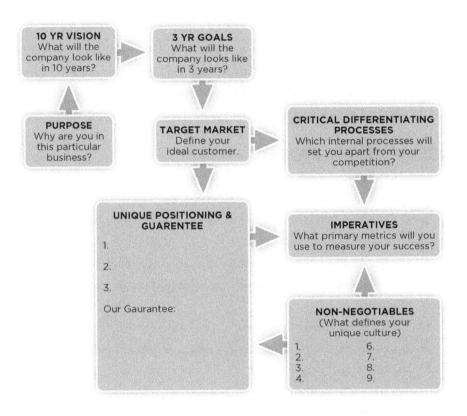

10 YR VISION
What will the company look like in 10 years?

3 YR GOALS
What will the company looks like in 3 years?

PURPOSE
Why are you in this particular business?

TARGET MARKET
Define your ideal customer.

CRITICAL DIFFERENTIATING PROCESSES
Which internal processes will set you apart from your competition?

UNIQUE POSITIONING & GUARENTEE
1.
2.
3.
Our Gaurantee:

IMPERATIVES
What primary metrics will you use to measure your success?

NON-NEGOTIABLES
(What defines your unique culture)
1.   6.
2.   7.
3.   8.
4.   9.

1 YEAR PLAN
End Date:
Revenue Target:
Profit Target:
CS Target:

THIS QUARTER'S PLAN
End Date:
Revenue Target:
Profit Target:
CS Target:

GOALS FOR THE YEAR
1.
2.
3.
4.
5.
THEME/FOCUS:

KPI'S - KEY PREDICTIVE INDICATORS
What will you measure on a weekly basis to predict future results?

CURRENT PRIORITIES
1.
2.
3.
4.
5.

PARKING LOT
What ideas have surfaces that you will prioritize later?

ISSUES THAT MUST BE RESOLVED
1.   5.
2.   6.
3.   7.
4.   8.

- **Vision (Where):** (1) Give a Brief Overview of You *10-year vision.* (2) Include your *3-year vision* as well. For both, *how big do you want it to be? What industries and markets are you in? What do you provide?*
- **Performance Standards (How):** Include a summary of your performance standard phrase or word so that your team can get on board with this.

PAGE ONE OF YOUR STRATEGIC SUMMARY

On page one of your strategic summary you'll find sections for your target market, critical business processes, imperatives, non-negotiables, and your guarantee. We will cover these later in the book, but here is a quick overview:

- **Target Market:** You must define your ideal customer, or avatar. You'll use this section to document critical characteristics about your ideal customer.
- **Critical Business Processes:** Every business has critical business processes that must be repeatedly and consistently performed. These are the critical processes you MUST execute flawlessly in order to out-perform your competition.
- **Your Imperatives:** You'll need some specific ways to measure your business's success. These are *your imperatives.* They provide a measuring stick to assess the performance of your business.
- **Your Non-Negotiables:** Every business has a culture. Your culture is determined by those elements of behavior you consider to be *non-negotiable.* You will list yours here.
- **Your Guarantee:** Your strategic summary should also include your unique positioning and your *guarantee.* This speaks to how you separate yourself from your competition in terms of your selling proposition, products, services, features and/or performance. It describes how you stand behind your product or service in a way that gives your customer confidence you're the right person to do business with.

Hopefully you can see how all this fits together strategically to summarize your business. You may need additional or different sections for your particular business. As you work through the book, feel free to add other elements critical to *your* business into your summary.

PAGE TWO OF YOUR STRATEGIC SUMMARY

Page two of your strategic summary is more tactical. It's all about your immediate plans. For this page, I recommend three sections: (1) what you're doing this quarter, (2) what you're doing this year, and (3) what you need to tackle in the future. Eventually, this will cover all the goals, action items, and deliverables you want to work on—the metrics by which to track your business's progress.

In business, you'll always have things that may be important but not immediate. Page two helps you focus on priorities in the right order to manage your time and focus on the things your business needs. There may be some things that are a bit further off in the future. That's fine, just park them in that section. Additionally, there may be some pressing issues that must be addressed as soon as possible. These go in this quarter's section. This way you can organize tasks for this quarter, this year, and so forth.

The goal is to completely describe everything about your business—where you are right now, where you are going, why, and how you plan to get there in a quick two pages. I'm not a big fan of writing a formal business plan. They are not that useful for a small business. They typically find a spot on a shelf and are rarely opened once written. You need something active, useful, and easily visualized that will be handy to refer to when people need it.

USING YOUR STRATEGIC SUMMARY MOVING FORWARD

As we move through this book and as you run your business, work on the sections on page two little by little. You may have some thoughts now, *great!* Put them in there. You can always refine it later.

Spend some time with your Strategic Summary and become familiar with it. Jot down your ideas as you go and don't be afraid to amend or edit them as you learn. Remember, *this is a work in progress.* This won't be finished until we're done with the book. I promise you, the more that you work with this strategic summary the more you're going to believe in it. When you share it with your team, they'll go, "Wow! I get it! I understand now what you mean when you say, 'Here's what we want to do and here's why."

Never again will your team sit there wondering, *why am I doing this?* They'll know why because it fits into the strategic summary. For now, put together what you can and keep it handy as we'll refer to it several times throughout the rest of the book. When we are finished, you'll have a complete document you're proud of. One that is inspirational, motivational, and that lets people know exactly what to do. *That's* your strategic summary.

SECTION THREE

THE STRUCTURE & FRAME OF YOUR BUSINESS

Chapter 14

BUSINESS STRUCTURE & FRAMEWORK

My dad wasn't all that interested in this topic. He was confident in his ability to know what to do when the unexpected came up. As a result, *there was no structure in his business.*

Dad's idea of a business was finding his own work, deciding what to charge and when to work, spending time with each customer ensuring they were satisfied, and ultimately collecting his fee once we were finished. It was no more complicated than that for Dad.

He didn't formally register his business. The IRS never knew about it, nor did the state ever see a formal business document from Allen & Sons Window Washing. That wasn't important to Dad. He also didn't worry about customer complaints and likely didn't know there was a Better Business Bureau. He didn't own much, so "protecting his assets" wasn't a priority either. But today things are very different than they were for my dad.

Today, it's essential to have business documents registered and up to date. Your business reputation matters as well—what with social media and instant world-wide communication. Structure is more critical than ever *because today's consumers have far more choices available right at their fingertips.* Competitors are on every corner. Today, you must be solid in your structure and framework or you'll never survive, let alone thrive.

I'm not sure Dad would like the way it works today. He enjoyed playing "fast and loose" in a way that now would drive a business right into the ditch. I want better than that for you; I don't want you to just get by. I want your business to be a powerful tool you use to achieve the goals you set in section one. In this section, I'm going to show you how to do that.

Chapter 15

YOUR FOUNDATION: BUSINESS DOCUMENTS

W e're now talking about your bike's frame, the structure of your business. When we think of a bike, the frame has one very important job: holding the wheels, handlebars, seat, and everything else together.

The same is true for your business, it's what holds all the different elements together. So just like with a bike, your business's frame *must be secure* because it's what *everything else is built on*. If it's not secure, *nothing in your business ever will be!*

The foundation of your business structure, or frame, is perhaps the most important. Your essential business documents make up the foundation, so they need to be securely in place. I'm well aware this is not a sexy topic. So I'm not going to give dull, legal advice. That's not our goal with your business documents. Instead, I want to pause long enough here to ensure you have the formal documentation you need to be fully prepared for the day you intend to exit your business.

We all exit our businesses one day, so preparing for it makes perfect sense. Making sure you can one day leave your business successfully is one of your important jobs. In fact, this just might be the start of your retirement plan. Why leave anything so important to chance? Why risk your most valuable asset? This would simply be foolishness.

> **TUNE-UP TIP:** Once again, I'll give you my disclaimer that I'm a business man offering business advice, not an attorney offering legal advice. Your formal business documents will need to address legal issues about which you should secure advice from a qualified business attorney. If for any reason you've not gone over your business documents with an attorney, do so as soon as possible—especially if you have partners or employees.

I know this stuff is dry, so let's be quick. However, don't let that fool you into thinking this isn't important. Here are four specific documents that you should have in place for your business:

1. **Formally Filed Legal Business Documents**
2. **A Written Operating Agreement**
3. **Partnership Agreement**
4. **A Written Exit Strategy**

Make sure you go over these with your team of advisors (including your attorney). That Team of Advisors exercise wasn't just for fun. You need them on this one to make sure you've got a solid foundation of business documents for your business's structure. One that will make your business successful today as well as during any period of transition in the future. It is true in business as in life—you just never know what's coming, so you better be prepared. Let's look a bit more closely at these four documents before moving on.

FORMALLY FILED BUSINESS DOCUMENTS

I strongly suggest you formally file your business as a unique entity other than just yourself. If not, you're putting yourself, your family, and your assets at risk.

What structure is right for you? Without getting bogged down into the legal differences between types of business structures, let's go over a few things you should research so you can make that decision wisely. One structure you should certainly research is a Limited-Liability Corporation, or LLC. Others you may want to research and talk to your attorney about include both an S Corporation and C Corporation.

So who should you talk to? Consult with your **CPA, business attorney, and financial planner** to help identify the right structure for your business. Ultimately you need a formally filed set of documents that provides your business legally sound structure. This will give it far greater stability, particularly when exiting the business, over using your personal assets as the structure.

This is job #1 for your business's structure. It just has to be in place to provide you, your family, and your personal assets adequate legal protection. What's more, the structure you choose will have *specific and ongoing annually required updates* in order for you to maintain that status, so factor that into your planning.

TUNE-UP TIP: Be prepared for the commitment your structure will require. It might mean member meetings, documented recordings of transactions, or any number of other obligations. Understand the requirements of your chosen formal business structure going in to ensure you remain solidly within them. Definitely enlist your attorney and other advisors on this.

Without formal protection, or if you negate it by co-mingling personal and business funds, you and your family's personal assets may be at risk. That's not why you went into business for yourself, so don't risk it. Do this before you do anything else with your business structure.

FORMAL OPERATING AGREEMENT

Once your formal business structure is in place, focus on a *formal operating agreement* that outlines (1) how decisions get made, and (2) who has what authority in your business. This is a legal document, so yes it's binding and it *will* protect you. It's a *good* thing. It helps everybody, yourself included, in a leadership position in your business to understand what triggers what activity, under what conditions things can and should be done, and under which other conditions they should not and cannot.

This agreement needs to be fairly comprehensive and cover many aspects of your business. You could start by downloading an operating agreement template, but I highly recommend getting your team of advisors in on this.

> **TUNE-UP TIP:** When's the best time to tackle the operating agreement? Good question! I've learned: the best time to undertake this task is when your business is not in turmoil. In reality, what that means is it's best to do this right up front before you get too far into things or some disagreement will spring up when you don't expect it. So avoid this trap and get this done right away.

PARTNERSHIP AGREEMENTS

If you have partners in your business, it's imperative that you have a *formal partnership agreement* that makes it easy to understand voting rights, who makes what decisions, and what authority limits exist. It's also great if a partner leaves the business (voluntarily or involuntarily). Be honest—you really never know when that might happen.

A partnership agreement helps partners reach an agreement before hand—when you are thinking clearly and no pressure is involved. It details how you intend to split different aspects of the business, like:

- What each partner does in the business
- What authorities partners have and share
- What to do if somebody has a medical condition arise
- What to do if a partner wants to leave the business
- What to do if a partner cannot cover their financial obligations to the business

If you have a partnership, have this agreement in place beforehand. No matter how well you get along with your partner, your partnership will have rough times. It doesn't matter if you are husband and wife or friends from college. It doesn't matter if it's two partners or five. Tension will come, and when it comes, this document will help resolve disputes, bring consensus, and ultimately protect your business. Even if the tension comes from an external source, your agreement will help prepare you for how to handle it.

Look, we all know life can and will happen so we must protect what's important to us. *Your business and partnership are no different.* As you work through your agreement, outline every potential scenario. Get it all out on the table and then down into the agreement. This is your third most important document following your formal business filing and operating agreement.

A WRITTEN EXIT STRATEGY

Before you say anything, *trust me*—it's never too early to start writing your exit strategy. You will exit your business one day, why not have a specific plan in mind? Doing so can provide tremendous benefits to you, your business, and your family.

An exit plan is clearly not a short term strategy and will need to change over time. However, *don't wait!* If you do, you may fall into the all-too-common trap of failing to plan your transition at all. Without doing this now, when you finally decide you want out, you'll be looking at 4–5 years of work to get the maximum value from your business.

So instead, I want you to plan out the best exit possible up front and keep that as your ultimate business goal until it is clear that a change is necessary. Remember back in Chapter 8 when I told you that your job was to create, compound, protect, distribute and ultimately transfer value? This is that transferring of value. This is how you ensure maximum ROI on your business when you go to sell. This *never* happens by accident. You must plan it to be ready when the time comes.

Start writing down your thoughts on how you'd like to exit when the time comes. You may find this even impacts the type of formal business structure you choose for your business. That's why this is one of the four foundational business documents for your business's frame.

LOOKING AHEAD

So no boring legal advice like I promised. However, you still need to go have those conversations with your accountant, lawyer, or other advisors. Take your time getting the advice you need. It's vitally important to consider these documents.

Though I gave you a list of four, there may be other documents your business needs to have a secure frame. If so, get them locked down as well. Without them, your frame will never provide your business the stability it needs to succeed.

Chapter 16

ORGANIZATION STRUCTURE

Many business owners don't or won't use formal organization charts. Turns out, these owners usually had a bad experience in a highly-structured organization in the past (more bureaucratic than helpful). To them, organizational structure only got in the way, *dis*connecting instead of connecting the different operations and functions of the business. I understand this fear, but what I have in mind for you is very different.

Individuals *want* to know what their responsibilities are, where they fit in the organization, and particularly *that there are opportunities for them to grow and expand with the company.* In a large organization, the room to move up is already apparent. But in a small business, the organization is often very flat. As you grow, an organization structure can show your employees the internal opportunities they have for promotion.

Our goal here is making crystal-clear to your team: (1) how everybody relates to one another, and (2) the opportunities for them to grow and expand in the future. Keep this in mind as you set out to define what your organization looks like.

A SIMPLE ORGANIZATION CHART

Let's do a little exercise and draw a simple organization structure. Let's start by imagining that your organization looks something like this:

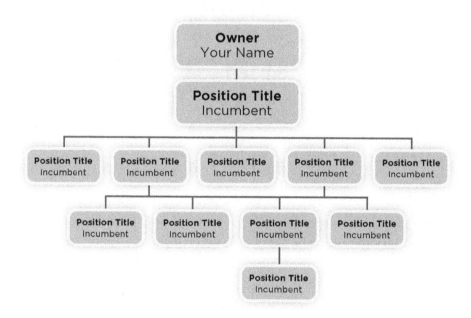

Now, notice that this organization chart is structured by *functional role or activity*, not by *individual*. This means a single person in your business (including yourself) who fulfills more than one functional role (for example, marketing *and* sales), will appear in more than one box on your organization chart. At first, you may only have one or two people, so their names may be in *several* boxes across your chart.

Now, draw your own chart with the activities required to run *your* business. But here's a twist—*draw your chart as if your business had achieved your year three vision.* Yes, draw the organization that would be needed in three years to support your now much larger organization. So include all functions and activities that do not currently exist, but will likely be in place in three years. For example, if you'll have an IT function, add the box even if you have no current IT staff.

As you draw, make each function a separate box *even if they are currently performed by the same person.* Once each function has a spot, start putting the names in the boxes. So one person, say Sally, may have her name in several boxes, including:

- Operations Activities
- Purchasing Activities
- Shop Operations
- Finance & Bookkeeping
- Human Resources
- And so forth…

You may have Sally doing multiple functions, especially if you are small. You yourself may be general manager, bookkeeper, and hiring manager. So put your name down in all three spots. Leave the boxes blank for functions that don't exist yet or write in "future" as a placeholder.

What Happens When You Do This

Hopefully you're getting a sense of how your business will look in three years. Here are a couple of key benefits from doing this you don't want to miss:

1. **You can now see which positions you will need to hire next.** Your future-looking organization chart helps you identify which position to fill *and* in what order to fill them. By looking at which roles will be critical first, you can plan your hiring order.

2. **Your team members can see the potential growth opportunities in your business.** This will motivate them to begin acquiring the skills to advance internally. *Don't under estimate how powerful a message this can be to your team.*

TUNE-UP TIP: I've got one more suggestion for your organization chart to make this clearer: Put a box at the top of the chart for the owner. This will allow you to define specifically (which will become really important next chapter) your role as the owner in contrast to your role as the general or operations manager of the business.

I hope you can see now that your organization's structure is much more complicated than you realized. This exercise allows you to identify *functional areas of opportunity* which will help you know exactly where and how to grow.

YOUR ORGANIZATION CHART AND YOU, THE BUSINESS OWNER

Now that you have your organization chart, start thinking of the different roles that you yourself are playing within your business, typically: (1) owner & (2) operating manager. These are *vastly different roles from one another.* Now, I'll talk more about this later, but I bring it up now to make the point that this chart will help prevent you from falling into the trap of only thinking of yourself as either manager *or* owner when instead *you are filling both roles.*

Hopefully you clearly see how creating your organization chart this way really does provide clarity:

1. It gives you a future-looking position to keep your thoughts on moving forward.
2. It allows you to put people into functions, instead of giving functions to people.
3. It charts your future growth and hiring.

This organization structure allows you to communicate clearly to your team; it's the frame of your bike—how you make sure every part of your business is *securely connected* to ensure it stays firmly together when you hit those inevitable bumps in the road of life.

Chapter 17

POSITION AGREEMENTS

E ach box on your new org chart represents a unique set of *responsibilities*. Normal organization charts, however, put the focus on individuals and their *job description*. A typical description includes required background, training, skill sets, and education. It communicates competencies and skills, *but does not address the critical issue of accountability.*

Job descriptions indeed have their place—they are extremely useful for hiring by helping you quickly identify if you are selecting the right people to interview for your team. They definitely have value. However, they're not good at defining the specific activities or functions that must be performed in your business.

You need a different tool to do this. That's why we're discussing "position agreements" in this chapter—to help you draw a distinction between them and traditional job descriptions. So let's look at how they are different and how that will help you implement your new organizational chart.

WHAT IS A POSITION AGREEMENT?

So now that we know what it's not, let's talk about what a position agreement actually is:

(Your Logo)

Business Name
Position Agreement

Job Title: _____

Name of Incumbent: _____

SUMMARY

This position is primarily responsible for

ESSENTIAL DUTIES include the following. Other duties may be assigned.

I understand that in this role, I will be accountable for the following.

- (list the things this position is resonsible to accomplish - be specific)
-
-
-
-

SUCCESS MEASURES

I understand that my success in fulfilling this position will be based on the following:

- (list the things this position will be measured on - be specific)
-
-

NON-NEGOTIABLES

I understand that in order to hold this or any other position within the company I must demonstrate the following key behaviors and traits:

- (list the Non-negotiables for you business)
-
-
-
-
-
-

AGREEMENT

I accept the responsibilities, duties and measures assigned to the position.

Signed: _____   Dated: _____

As the template demonstrates, a position agreement is **structured differently** than a job description, so it's better at communicating *what's expected, what you must accomplish, and how you will be measured.* There are four critical elements of a position agreement:

1. **What I Am Responsible For**
2. **Performance Metrics**
3. **Specific Behaviors That Must Be Demonstrated**
4. **Commitment To The Position**

WHAT AM I RESPONSIBLE FOR?

The first component put's the focus not on *what someone does,* but on what processes they are *responsible for.* This first section answers the question, "What areas must I take ownership of?" **Taking responsibility for a function instead of doing a task is one of the key differences between a job description and a position agreement.**

This part of the position agreement is where you go beyond saying, "You're going to answer the phones." Instead, a position agreement says, "You're responsible for ensuring people have a great impression when they call in and for how that gets handled." It's the "responsible for" piece that transforms your business with everyone knowing their personal responsibilities.

Additionally, this section outlines what people must do to make sure these things happen as they should. This helps people think in terms of responsibilities as they define for themselves how to do this—giving them ownership ensuring they *clearly know* what they are responsible to do.

PERFORMANCE METRICS

Position agreements next need to define the *performance metrics* used to measure performance. This answers questions like, "How will I be measured? What results should the person responsible for this produce?" Performance metrics are vital. Every position needs a set of performance metrics assigned to its functions. Have daily performance measurements for all positions if possible. Some won't need this, but someone in sales or operations could easily have daily metrics. Include weekly and monthly performance metrics as well if this is possible.

Metrics need to specifically define:

1. What you expect of your employee on a daily basis.
2. What you expect each week.
3. What you expect each month.

This is your way to communicate, "Here's what I expect. You're responsible for these things, and I'm going to measure your performance on these specific outcomes."

SPECIFIC BEHAVIORS

The third part of a position agreement should outline the two types of behaviors you need to consider:

1. **General Behaviors:** These are behaviors you expect all team members to display. In construction, you may want to cover safety behaviors. In retail, customer service goes here. These may be worded specifically to the position to help employees clearly understand how these general behaviors translate to their unique responsibilities.
2. **Position Specific Behaviors:** There may also be a few positions that require unique behaviors for a specific function. Here's where you communicate these specifically.

COMMITMENT TO THE POSITION

At the bottom of each position agreement is a signature section for both the team member and their supervisor. This sets a position agreement apart from a traditional job description. It is a pact between the individual and their supervisor. There's something about requiring someone to sign a document that makes expectations about accountability 100% real and transparent. Once signed, the document should be part of the person's personnel record. Don't leave this section off! It is a powerful part of the accountability system your business needs.

A Mental Exercise

Imagine if everybody in your business knew what they were responsible for and clearly understood that *as a result of being responsible for this specific area, I must do these things on a regular basis to ensure this responsibility is fulfilled. I'll be measured on these specific things, so I need to do them every day.*

What *would* it be like if everyone had this clearly laid out for them? How well would your business function with such clarity? How much more profitably would your business be if this were the case? You'd likely see *massive* improvement if everybody knew these things about their position. Utilizing position agreements the easiest way to get you there!

A STEP-BY-STEP PROCESS TO IMPLEMENTING POSITION AGREEMENTS

1. **Start With Your Own Position Agreement.** These are for every position in your business, starting with you. What are you responsible for as the owner? How will you measure your performance?

2. **General/Operations Manager Position Agreement.** Next, set your general/operations manager agreement. What are they responsible for? What are their required behaviors and performance metrics?

3. **Create One for Every Other Position.** Once these are set, you tell your employees, "I've got my set of activities and you have yours. They are different, but we all have them. They all relate to one another and work together."

4. **Make sure all position agreement documents are signed.** Every position agreement should be signed by the person in that position and their supervisor. If everybody on your team reports to you, you have to sign them all. The supervisor must agree to be accountable for this as well.

5. **Post your Position Agreements.** If you really want to be bold, post these agreements where everyone can read them. There's nothing in them that needs to be confidential. No compensation or benefits are mentioned, so you can make them public. This is a powerful way that

makes it easy for people to see if something's missing that perhaps still needs someone responsible for it.

This is a powerful tool to turn a typically mundane task-oriented job description into a game-changing way to strengthen your business's framework. This will go a long way to making sure that every nut, bolt, and piece of your business is rock solid like you want.

Chapter 18

ACCOUNTABILITY

O nce you have your organization chart and positioning agreements in place, the question now becomes: *How do you hold people accountable for the things you assigned to them?* How do you establish *accountability* in your business on a consistent and powerful basis?

Many business owners fall short with accountability. This most likely happens because they become distracted. They get focused on their tasks and forget the important role of *installing systems that ensure others do what they are responsible to do.*

Let's look at a couple of tools you can use to help in this area. Like always, I encourage you to try a few things until you find the accountability tool that's right for *you.* It does not need to be anything complex. It may be a document everyone can access or a common business app like Trello, Smartsheets, or Basecamp. Anything that works for you is fine.

THE SIX-BY-SIX METHOD

One method is called the *six-by-six.* This is simply a method and a mindset. All that is required is a simple Excel file.

Here's how it works: *each individual in the business identifies the six priorities or critical tasks they will focus on over the next six weeks.* This could be project strategies, areas of focus—whatever fits your business. The important part is having *six specific things you're working on over the next six weeks.* As you maintain your "six-by-six," you ensure you accomplish a certain number of things in a specific timeframe.

A six-by-six helps you accomplish tasks and *move your business forward.* For this to work, these six things need to be broken down into small, describable, and distinct action items that can be tracked and measured. The more your team can accomplish, the faster your business moves and grows.

Your six-by-six is simple and should look something like this:

#	Item/Project Name	Complete?	Status / Details
1.	Annual Inventory	No	Nearly Done: 8/10 Categories Finished
2.	Warehouse Reorganization	No	New Shelving Ordered for Cat. 1–5. Need larger shelving for large item storage.
3.	Rebuild loading dock	Yes	Reported completion to Sally on 3/14
4.	Etc.		
5.	Etc.		
6.	Etc.		

You just need (1) the project name, (2) whether or not it's complete, and (3) a place for pertinent details. That's really all there is to it: a simple chart with a number of activities and their duration to help people maintain focus on what they're doing.

TUNE-UP TIP: If you are thinking, *I don't want to do this six-by-six thing. I think for me, a four-by-four or even two-by-two would be better*, you're probably right! The size of your grid doesn't really matter! What's important is that it works for you. If you get two things done in two weeks, that's progress! Find something that works and use it!

What the Six-by-Six Method Will Do for You

There are many benefits to a six-by-six. Why do a performance evaluation when you've got a detailed list of everything everyone on your team did for the past year? *Just look at their six-by-six!* Other dimensions of performance definitely matter, but with a six-by-six, there's no need to reconstruct the history of what your team did *because it's all right there for you on their accountability sheet*—talk about quick and easy! Here's what you need to do:

- **Find the right tool**: Get your *Six-by-Six, Four-by-Four, Three-by-Five*, or whatever you are going to use for your business set.
- **Direct report weekly accountability meeting:** Hold weekly meetings with everyone on your team that works directly for you.
- **Team weekly accountability meetings**: Beyond your own meetings, anyone else who has direct reports needs to hold weekly meetings to make sure their teams are moving forward on projects, assigned activities, and responsibilities.

This *will* develop real accountability in your business. One of my mentors used this methodology with his 11 direct reports. Every week he held these meetings without fail and the results were incredible. This is a great model for you to follow.

These weekly meetings are both (1) a tool to track what's going on with projects, and (2) a weekly review that guarantees accountability. Start with short meetings. They don't have to be 45 minutes long. Twenty or thirty minutes is more than enough at first. You just need a short, standup meeting so everyone knows this matters to you. This does two specific things for you:

1. **It creates great alignment.** You'll find the activities that get done in your business are *in alignment with your strategy and where you want to go!* Instead of people wasting time on things that don't move the needle, they'll be driving your business forward. That's the goal: having your team working on *the things that matter to your 10-year vision.*

2.   **It creates a powerful notion of consistency**. If everyone in your business knows that you're a leader who understands where they're going, defines their roles, gives them a way to keep track of activities, and checks in on them on a regular basis, then they are going to step up and do what you want done. They will see you value their efforts, your consistency, and the rigor in your business, and they *will* respond because they will understand this is what makes your business *powerful.*

Alignment and consistency are lacking in many businesses. This will be one discipline that will allow you to truly differentiate yourself from other businesses.

Find The Right Accountability Tool For Your Business

It's time to *find your accountability tool.* If the template above works, *use it!* If it doesn't, *modify it,* or *use a tool that works better for you!* This is a simple but *critical* process to the structure or frame of your business. It *must* be in place for your bike to be able to move with certainty. So make sure *everybody* knows what they're doing and has a way to track their progress.

SECTION FOUR

WINNING CUSTOMERS

Chapter 19

WINNING NEW CUSTOMERS

Many small businesses struggle finding enough new customers. These businesses typically do so because: (1) they do not generate a sufficient flow of leads, or (2) they have no process in place to convert leads into paying customers. As a result, even though they have a solid product or a great service, they just don't have the customers they need to consistently grow and expand their business.

My dad certainly had his issues with customers, but winning them over wasn't one of them. He was a *natural* when it came to this. He excelled in situations that normally scared off even the best salesmen. Dad would look for the biggest house or estate in the neighborhood and just go right up and introduce himself. To him, it was a game to see if he could get past the gate-keeper (usually the maid or groundskeeper), speak to the lady of the house, and then come away with a sale—which meant it was time to go to work. And boy was he good at it!

I specifically remember one time when we stopped in front of a particularly huge estate. It literally looked like a castle to me at the time. The owners (who we didn't yet know) were the Ratners. Dad stopped, gazed over and feasted his eyes upon seemingly hundreds of leaded, stained-glass windows. They were *very* ornate, which meant they were difficult to clean. To my dad, *the challenge was on!*

He grabbed his Big Chief tablet and quickly hurried up the long driveway, determined to meet the lady of the house. As we waited in the van, neighbors walked by frowning and staring. *What are THEY doing in this neighborhood?* It was pretty clear we were sorely out of place. They didn't like us just hanging around in a van, casing the joint. But we had no choice. Meanwhile, Dad made it to Ms. Ratner herself, and in his smooth, confident, and enthusiastic way, he had convinced her she needed our help.

So we waited as Ms. Ratner took Dad around the estate looking at windows, gutters, outdoor lights, chandeliers, you name it. He convinced her he could clean any and everything! He came back with a huge Cheshire cat-like grin and said, "Grab your ladders boys—we're going to work!" And so it began. The Ratner's became one of my dad's most loyal and consistent customers. He did *anything* for them, *no matter what*. He always found a way to get what they needed done. The result? *They treated him like he was part of their family.*

I could tell you a dozen more stories about my dad and other families. Each time, Dad somehow found work without planning it. He had no website or cell phone. He simply got out of his van, walked up the driveway, knocked on the door and was so over-the-top confident that the he turned skeptical homeowners into faithful customers right there on the spot. No, it wasn't difficult for Dad to ask people for the business, *because he knew there was no one who could match his commitment, his dedication, his attention to detail, or his price.*

What I want you to take from my dad's experience here is that winning customers is more than science—it's also an art. More than anything, Dad taught me the importance of *self-confidence and commitment*. If you know your customer well, speak to them directly & confidently, and don't be afraid to ask for the business, you *will*, just like my dad, always be able to win new customers.

Chapter 20

YOUR AVATAR

I want to start by convincing you of the importance for you to own this part of your business. This is one of those critical areas that the business owner, *must* take complete ownership of in order to succeed. By that, I mean *do not outsource this to someone else. **Do this yourself, at least in the beginning of your business adventure!***

Too many business owners *outsource* their front wheel. They find a hired gun to do this and as a result—they never really "own" anything. All they really do is "rent" someone's knowledge instead of building a sustainable business of their own. What happens when the person they depend on for their success leaves? With them goes everything needed to sustain their business—leaving the owner with *nothing.*

We're going to take your front wheel apart carefully and look at it piece by piece so that you can make thoroughly sound decisions in this area. We'll dive deep into each component to be certain you see how they work together. When we're done, you'll be able to engage with people who know nothing about your business and bring them to a place where they are comfortable with you and genuinely believe your business is special. From here, it'll be easy for them to decide to give you their business over and over again.

DEFINING YOUR AVATAR

First, we need to *define your avatar*. This is the center part of the front wheel of your bike, or *the hub*. This is the part of the wheel that attaches to the frame, the part that connects everything on your front wheel. The spokes, the rim, and the tire. Everything extends from the hub—where you define your avatar, your ideal customer.

When I say avatar, imagine with me a very specific person who embodies the characteristics, traits, behaviors and attitudes of your "dream" customer. I want you to visualize them standing or sitting in the room right there with you.

Now, your first thought might be, *I've got several different types of customers. All shapes and sizes!* You're right—that is true, I'm not denying this.

However, I still want you to speak directly and powerfully to *one person*—the one who *best* represents your perfect customer. You need to know them so you can get inside their head and understand their feelings, concerns, and priorities. This is crucial to your front wheel.

TUNE UP TIP: Flood Lights vs Lasers. Let's use an analogy to help you relate to your real-world customers. Think about a light. Imagine a *flood light* illuminating a room. It casts a broad light with *very little power to penetrate.* So it's good for adequately lighting an area, but not to provide illumination across great distances.

Now imagine light so focused and penetrating that it's a laser. It doesn't light up the room, but it can burn right through physical objects and be seen from miles away. This is what you want with your focus on your messaging to your ideal customer. You want your message to penetrate through all the marketing noise and speak directly to them. The only way to do that is to know exactly who you're trying to talk to.

Let's spend some time getting deeply familiar with your *ideal customer*. I've got an exercise focused on asking questions and considering how specific issues relate to your *ideal* customer. It's a great tool to learn as much as possible about how your ideal customer thinks and feels. So let's shine your laser right at them.

Grab your journal and start to answer some of the questions you need to ask about your avatar, or ideal customer.

DEMOGRAPHICS

Start with the basics, your avatar's demographics. You want to understand things about them like:

- Income Range
- Neighborhood
- Ethnicity
- Age
- Education Level
- Where they shop
- The type of car they drive
- What style of clothes they wear

These details help you physically pinpoint your ideal customer. This could easily take up an entire page in your journal. Be specific. Go beyond "anybody interested in buying a home," "people who like to eat," or, "somebody who owns a car." That's not deep enough. You need to move beyond superficial information and *into age range, income level, neighborhood, personal shopping preferences, and so on.* Get as specific as possible about distinguishing outward characteristics.

TRY TO UNDERSTAND THEIR FRUSTRATIONS

Next, and this is more important than demographics, really dig into their frustrations. List all the things you think of because there is probably more than one. For each issue, you might need a sub-list.

I take my clients through this exercise all the time. If they only come up with one page of ideas, I tell them, "We're not done. We've got to think deeper. We've got to think more because this is how we're going to crystallize our messaging." So think deeply about what truly frustrates them.

Ask yourself what bothers them so much they lose sleep. You know when something is on your mind and you just can't sleep? Your ideal customer is human and experiences this too, so ask yourself: what keeps them up at night and is it something you could help with?

Think about your industry. What's most frustrating about it? When your ideal customer does business with people in your line of work (maybe your competition and other alternatives that they have), what is it that they are most concerned about going wrong?

It might be *pain, frustration, concern or apprehension*, but we need to understand the biggest issue that they have so you can build a product or service that solves it—that's the goal.

DIVE EVEN DEEPER

Beyond what they are worried about, you need to dive even deeper and uncover things that your ideal customer may not even be aware of yet. You're the one with the unique insight they lack. What is it that they may not have encountered yet that you are aware of, and what can you do to protect them from experiencing this?

What about their hopes? Take a second here and think about the good as well as the bad. This is the upside of the equation—what your ideal customer hopes they can accomplish and who they can become. You need to understand what inspires them.

So ask, *what are their hopes? What are their goals, dreams, and aspirations?* Get inside their heart and mind for a minute and consider their hopes.

Just like there are bad things they don't know, there are good things your ideal customer is unaware of as well. Likely, they're so stuck in their pain that they've come to a point where they say, "Forget it, I'll just live with it." I hear that all the time, don't you?

That's not good enough for your customers, however. You want to show them it *can* and *should* be better without that pain. So think hard: *what opportunity lies ahead that they don't yet recognize? What can you do to help them realize potential they aren't yet thinking about?*

JOURNAL YOUR RESPONSE

Spend time journaling your response to these questions. The goal is *go deep*—three to four pages of detail is not unreasonable:

What are their demographics?

What are their frustrations?

What keeps them awake at night?

What worries them about your industry?

What unknown issues don't they see?

What are their hopes?

What opportunities don't they see?

You want as clear a picture as possible of what's inside their head. The clearer you are, the deeper you can go, and the easier everything else will become. Remember: *this is the core of winning customers.* With this set, your front wheel is secure and your business can move forward.

Chapter 21

CREATING AWARENESS

The next step to winning customers is *creating awareness* about your business, products, and services. We now must identify the ways you are going to get your message to the ideal customer we just defined. We call these different methods of reaching your ideal customer your *spokes*, or the *channels of communications* you use to create awareness.

To begin, we have to figure out how to interrupt your ideal customer's normal world of distractions, their phone, text messages, posts on Facebook, YouTube videos, or ads they see on TV—whatever it is that currently has their attention. We've got to find a way to get their attention away from this, which means we need to *pop* in some way. Here are a couple of ideas to consider:

3. **There is no S*ilver Bullet:* If you've heard, "You *MUST* do this specific strategy," don't listen. There just is no such thing as a silver bullet that works for every situation. Business just doesn't happen that way. Instead, *you must be willing to experiment*, or you're going to get stuck. Many business owners fall into the "only one approach works" marketing trap. They found one way that works, and even if it's not effective, they are sticking to it. If one day their way doesn't work, they say, "I must have a bad product," or "This business isn't for me," and they quit. The reality

is *no business works with a single, inflexible approach*. You *must* be willing to experiment.

4. **Experiment Wisely:** Now being willing to experiment is one thing, but don't just try things willy-nilly. No one has an infinite reserve of cash. You must be smart and test and measure everything you try. This is a fundamental business principle: *always test and measure*.

Let's cover the 5 fundamental rules for the spokes on your front tire:

RULE #1: YOU NEED MORE THAN TWO SPOKES

You cannot survive with just two spokes. Ever seen a bike tire with just two spokes? Of course not! The moment you hit a bump in the road the wheel would break. Two spokes *do not* provide enough stability to your front wheel for your bike to go anywhere.

Yet this happens *all the time*. Businesses try to save money by only using 1 or 2 marketing strategies. Unfortunately, if all you've done is put an ad in a local magazine or buy a Google AdWords campaign, *this isn't enough*. It *won't* sustain you when the inevitable "bumps in the road" come along. You need *at least 6-8 spokes* to provide the strength and security that keeps your front wheel from collapsing. That is, six to eight specific marketing strategies designed to speak directly to your avatar.

Start with this list here or any other ideas you already have. Some may be more relevant than others depending on your business, but this is a good start:

Magazine Advertising	Window Displays
Local Advertising	Testimonials
Building Signage	Videos
Vehicle Wrap	TV Advertising
Website Banner Ads	Radio Advertising
Google Ad Words	Strategic Alliance Partners
Social Media Campaigns	A Trade Show Booth
Billboards & Posters	Website Promotions
Direct Mail Campaigns	Etc.

If you're a new business owner just starting out, or if you have a limited marketing budget, you'll want to pick *one or two* ideas to begin with and then *build a schedule to add 1–2 more each month or quarter* until you reach 6–8 working spokes in your front wheel.

If you're an existing business, you will likely be able to identify 6–8 strategies right away. This list is just a few ideas to get you started. What's most important is finding the 6–8 *best strategies* for your specific business and unique avatar.

RULE #2: SET A BUDGET FOR EACH SPOKE

Identify how much you are willing to spend on each strategy over a predefined period of time. Unfortunately, you can't expect all of your marketing to be free. This will require an investment. So it is important to set a budget just like with any other part of your business.

What size budget? This can vary based on your industry and how far along you are with your business. A typical budget for a start-up business is usually around 8–10% of revenues. In a more established business, this might be closer to 4–5% of revenues. The bottom line is doing this effectively will require some investment. So you must make sure you are doing that wisely.

RULE #3: TEST YOUR MESSAGES

Now that you've set your budget, *test your messages*. Every time you do a marketing message, make sure that you're testing whether it is working or not. If it isn't, it's a waste of your resources and you need try something else.

Each message should have three parts: (1) a headline, (2) copy, and (3) a call to action. You can search online for "Headline Bank" to find headlines that have previously worked to catch people's attention. Often times, these idea banks are extremely useful.

You can take a headline that has worked well in some other industry and use it in your industry by making a couple of minor changes to it. This will save you from having to create your own unique and clever headlines. Save time by *using a headline someone else already tested and measured for you.* I strongly recommend this approach. Remember, headlines matter *a lot*. So you are going to need to test your headline, your copy, and your offer.

RULE #4: MEASURING YOUR RESULTS

As you test your messages, you'll need to *measure your results*. That is, you need a way to know whether or not your specific messages or marketing strategies are working. To do this, you'll first need some performance indicators. Include a CALL TO ACTION in your marketing messages to help with this. Do you want the reader to visit your website? Pick up the phone and call you? Click on a specific link, or what? Whatever it is, identify it and be prepared to measure how often your messaging makes that action happen.

You might measure website hits, phone calls, click-thru rates, or any number of things. But this is the beginning of *your dashboard* (more on this later). Over time, as you test & measure your specific marketing messages, you'll be able to define which really do generate the most awareness for your business.

RULE #5: MAKE CHANGES BASED ON DATA

The final rule is *make changes **based on the data** you collected from your tests and measurements*. All testing and measuring is for naught if you don't use the data in your future decision making. Always strive to ensure the changes you make are based upon data you are collecting from your previous efforts. This will allow you to shift dollars from one strategy to another. You may find it's better to double up on one that works and phase out a few that do not. You can even try completely new spokes if your measurements indicate you need a change.

As you make your marketing decisions based upon actual, documented results, you will begin making significant progress.

TUNE-UP TIP: As a business owner, I can assure you that you will get tired of your marketing messages far faster than your ideal customer or ideal prospect will. You've heard the message time and time again, but, in reality, your ideal customer has only heard it one or two times. So how do you avoid falling into a trap of prematurely changing your message? By following this rule: *don't make changes about your marketing simply based on your gut. Instead, only make changes based on collected data.*

SUGGESTIONS FOR FURTHER RESEARCH: JAY LEVINSON & GUERRILLA MARKETING

Jay Levinson is widely known as the *father of guerrilla marketing.* You can find his books by doing a Google search on his name or on the term "Guerrilla Marketing." Personally, I'm a big fan of Jay and his wisdom. I highly suggest you look into his work on creating awareness. He really was brilliant, probably one of the best at finding low-cost or no-cost ways to create awareness with strategies that still get terrific results.

For more, check out Jay Levinson's work, particularly *Guerrilla Marketing.* It's fantastic! One key from it I want to share is the saying, "It takes nine impressions to get someone to do business with you." That means, in order to catch someone's attention, you must get your message in front of them *at least nine times.*

Jay goes deeper, however, and also found **two out of every three times your message reaches your ideal customer, they're not even paying attention!** So only one out of every three times you think you are reaching your audience are you actually doing so! If you've been doing the math, this means: *you'll need to get your message in front your ideal customer at least **27 times** before you can expect them to respond and to take action.*

This means most people are not effective with advertising simply because they give up long before they ever get to the 27 impressions mark. This is just one example of the type of insights you'll find in Jay's work. Jay passed away recently, but his work is still some of the best out there on this topic.

LOOKING AHEAD

You've got a lot to do here. What's most important is that you don't give up! I want you to come at this methodically and strategically:

1. Identify your 6-8 marketing strategies.
2. Create a budget for each strategy.
3. Test your messaging with a call to action.
4. Measure your results to see how well your efforts are doing.
5. Make adjustments and changes based on the data as needed.

This process is *powerful* and will help you build a solid front wheel on your bike so that the front end of your business will be highly successful at getting your message to your ideal customer. That's what this is all about!

Chapter 22

EDUCATING
YOUR PROSPECTS

O ur next goal is describing the *tire* on the front wheel of your bike. This is where the rubber truly meets the road. And for your business, this is the process you use to *educate prospects* who respond to your marketing messages.

In today's marketplace, using education-based sales techniques are powerful. If you look, you can see them everywhere. Businesses are trying to help their prospects make informed buying decisions. So as we discuss turning prospects in to buyers, we will focus on education first.

Now if you are a business owner who thinks "selling" is a dirty word because of an experience you've had in the past, I want to steer you away from those negative thoughts. I want you to think about selling as a *respectable* way for you to *help your ideal customer make the best purchasing decision they can to meet their specific needs.*

In the final analysis, the right solution for your prospect may not be your product or service. If that's so, "sales" as I mean it says that you send them to find the best solution for their problem. Think of Zappo's. They are known for doing whatever it takes to find the *right* solution for their customers.

They'll literally talk to prospective customers for hours to help them solve their purchasing issues in any way possible. In the end, the solution may not involve a purchase from Zappo's, and that's fine with them! You need to adopt a similar approach. Make everything you do about educating and assisting your customer.

So how do you educate your prospects? You start by (1) *having a positive attitude about what selling is,* and (2) *focusing your conversations on helping people make good buying decisions.*

CREATING RECIPROCITY WITH YOUR PROSPECTS

There are many ways to educate prospects. One approach that works well is to give prospects something of value before you begin talking about your products or services. By *giving first* you activate the influence of *reciprocity*. Reciprocity is a natural reaction people have in interpersonal relations: if I give you something, you feel obliged to give me something back.

Giving away some of your knowledge is a powerful first step to building trust with your ideal prospect. They will naturally have a reciprocal reaction and take more interest in your business. The goal is to lead them to saying, "Wow! That was awfully nice of you. You did that for me? That's the kind of person I want to do business with!" That's how your sales staff should approach every potential selling opportunity.

You want your sales team thinking about helping your prospects. Whether the solution relates to your company, services, or products or not, if your team solves their issue, they'll remember it and tell people about you. That's what this is all about: winning new customers. So let's go over four fundamentals to consider as you begin educating your prospects:

1. Give Your Best Stuff Away
2. Wow Them
3. Use Multiple Touches
4. Achieve Ideal Positioning

GIVE YOUR BEST STUFF AWAY

Don't hold back your best stuff or keep it hidden! Instead, *give away your best stuff!* It makes people think, *Wow! There's a lot more there than I realized. If they're giving this away, there must be lot's more that I don't yet know!*

Now I don't mean that if you're a plumbing company you give away your water heaters. What I do mean is you should give away the knowledge of how to tell if a water heater is near the end of its life cycle. *Give away the tricks and techniques you use to extend the life of the water heater.*

If you give prospects your best ideas and the advice they need to do some things on their own, when the big thing comes up they can't handle, they'll call you first because they know you'll take good care of them. Giving them your best up front lets them know that *they matter to you and that you have their best interests in mind.*

So the first thing to do in terms of educating your prospects is *give them the good stuff.* I hope that when you started this book you felt like I gave you the good stuff. It was not my intention to hold anything back. I intend to share with you the entire blue print of what I believe it takes to run a successful, profitable business. You can take this on your own to do it by yourself, and many people do just that.

At some point, your prospects will encounter some difficulty or complication and hopefully they will think of you. I want you to share your best stuff and I want you to know and be confident that since you're the expert in your field, when they really need something significant, they'll come to you because you've proven that to them. So share your best stuff up front—just give it away!

"WOW" THEM

Next, I want you to *WOW them*, and I want you to do it for free. I say *free* because I don't want you to wait until *after* they become a customer. I want you to WOW them before. I want them to say, "WOW, why would you do that for me? Why would you just give me that?"

The more you can WOW your prospect right away without them feeling they have to purchase something from you, the more they're going to believe in who you are. You see it all over the place. The ones that make the biggest impact on their ideal customer are those that have thought, *what could I do to WOW them? What can I do to really blow their socks off?* Time and time again, *it works!*

USE MULTIPLE TOUCHES

Next, make sure your team knows educating a prospect doesn't happen in one conversation or meeting. This requires *multiple touches.* This isn't the kind of selling where you meet a customer and right away you're transacting business. It's not like that. In almost all cases, it is going to require multiple touches.

Remember *Guerilla Marketing?* Remember how you need to get your message in front of your ideal customer as many as 27 times in order for them to do business with you? Trying to close a sale in one touch is foolish. Instead, plan to do it in 9 touches as Jay recommends.

Don't waste your time trying to sell too early or you will only ruin a potentially good prospect. It happens quite often. Too many people just dive into the sales process before the prospect is even close to being fully educated.

Remember, this chapter is about *educating,* not selling. That's the focus: helping your prospects understand how to make a good buying decisions. Along the way, they'll come to understand how to make that good buying decision and think to themselves, "Geez, a lot of roads lead to these guys!" They are going to think this because you've been busy WOWing them by sharing your best and connecting with them again and again without forcing a sale.

ACHIEVE IDEAL POSITIONING

When you establish a multiple touch relationship, what you're really doing is giving yourself the opportunity do some *positioning* by giving them a great understanding of what doing business with you is like.

As you're educating prospects, sharing your best, finding ways to WOW them, and having multiple touches, what you are really truly doing is showing them: *when you do business with my company, this is how you'll be treated.* People really respond to this approach. One of the biggest fears they have is making a bad purchase decision. By educating them, you help them avoid making a hasty mistake.

Educating prospects lets you ideally position yourself so that they'll know exactly what they get when they do business with you. Before moving on, make sure you can answer the following questions for your business:

1. How can you trigger Reciprocity with your ideal prospects?
2. What are some things that you could share that are some of "Your Best Stuff?"
3. How could you WOW prospects? Come up with some ideas and get your team on board.
4. What are the Multiple Touches you will build into your process?

Once your prospects are educated, you'll be able to "ask for the business," which is our next topic.

Chapter 23
ASKING FOR THE BUSINESS

N ow it's time to turn your prospect into your customer. That means we need to talk about how to *ask them for their business*. This is one of those topics that *tons* of books cover. So no matter how deep we go here, realize this is just a scratch on the surface.

My goal here will be to help you get your mind in the right place rather than to give you a step-by-step process like we have the last few chapters. Here, your methodology *must* fit your specific business, beliefs, and culture. So let's peel back a few layers on the subject. Let's cover some of the key areas, tools, and resources that you'll need before you really dive into this topic on your own.

THERE IS NO SINGLE RIGHT WAY TO ASK FOR THE BUSINESS

Like your marketing strategy, there's no silver bullet or single right way that turns every prospect into a customer. People are different from one another, so you'll need different approaches in kind. Now, you may already have a favorite approach you are already using. I've personally read at least a dozen different approaches to asking for the business, and I've found elements of each that have merit and work. Here are a couple of options to get you started:

1. Jeffrey Gitomer has several books on this subject including the very popular, *The Sales Bible*. It's full of powerful and compelling sales techniques. I really like how he asks for the business. If you want something simple, powerful, yet a bit edgy, give Jeffrey a try.
2. For a slightly different approach, try *Spin Selling* by Neil Rackham. It's another one of my favorites.

Now, there are *many* books out there—not just these two, and I've listed some of them at the end of this book. For now, however, let's dive a bit more into the methodology of one book I really like: Daniel Pink's, *To Sell is Human*.

Daniel Pink's ABCs of Business

I like Daniel Pink because he dives deep into the *psychology of selling*. Daniel is a very insightful business author. *To Sell is Human* is just one of his books, but it's a tremendously insightful one with a fresh approach to asking for the business. Daniel starts with the old ABCs of selling: *Always Be Closing*. Then he drastically redefines what ABC stand for:

- **A = Attunement:** How do you tune in so that your customers know you're speaking directly to them? How do you attune yourself to your ideal customer so you can listen to and connect with them in a real way that they'll recognize?
- **B = Buoyancy:** In business, people are going to say no to you. That just happens. Buoyancy, therefore, is about learning to bounce back and stay afloat when others would give up. It's about learning to be okay with a prospect saying no.
- **C = Clarity:** This is clarity in *identifying a problem* your prospect may not even see. You want to help them clarify their needs when they may fail to understand their true problem.

So *attunement, buoyancy* and *clarity*. I love it! Simple, yet powerful way of thinking.

DIY: BUILDING YOUR SALES FUNNEL

No matter what anyone says, if you're going to ask for the business in a way you can own (which I highly recommend doing), you need a system that works for *you*. This has to be DIY. The alternative is hiring a sales hotshot to join your team on some highly commission-based compensation plan who may ultimately leave and take their sales process with them—leaving you with nothing.

Instead, *slowly build a thoughtful, step-by-step process that everyone at your company follows.* Why everyone? *Because if everyone doesn't follow it, it's not a process.* If it's not a process, it's random, and *you can't measure random.* Without measurement, you cannot make predictions. So it must be a process that everyone follows.

THE VACUUM CLEANER SALES-FUNNEL MODEL:
A STEP-BY-STEP PROCESS

Now I want to talk about the concept of a Sales Funnel for a moment before diving into specifics. You'll see below the common concept of a sales funnel with a large end at the top and the small end at the bottom:

As you can see, leads go into the top and somehow come out the bottom as customers. I don't think it works that way. I want to replace that image with something very different. Instead, I want you to picture the image on the next page—something more like a vacuum cleaner:

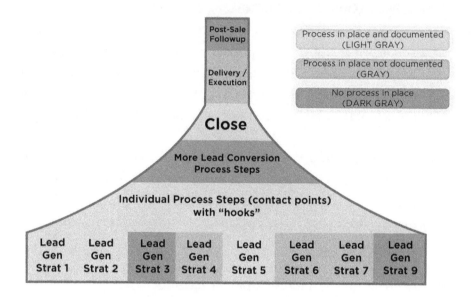

Here, things are drawn up from the bottom to the top. This is more representative of a true sales process. Your sales funnel is more like a vacuum cleaner where the head sucks up leads. These are your marketing strategies from the last chapter. This is how you attract prospects. They hear your message and are attracted by it much like how dirt in your carpet is attracted to the head of a vacuum.

Next comes a step-by-step process where you hook this lead and pull them through your sales funnel. Think of a fish on a fishing line. If someone enters your sales vacuum, the next step of the process is to have something *hook their attention*—an attention getter, something to wow them.

So the first two or three steps in the process are about educating your prospect with built in activities and *free stuff* that *wows* them. Doing this makes them want to learn more about you and thus move along the path towards becoming a customer.

Moving From Education To Sales

At some point in the process you will finally have the opportunity to have a sales conversation. At that moment you can start to share more details about your business, services, or products. This builds upon what we've already discussed—learning about your prospect and making sure they know what they need to know to make good buying decisions.

Once all the other elements are in place, it's time to start asking for the business. By that I mean *start to tell them how your company works, why you are special, and what it's like to do business with you.* This is where you can start to sell.

 TUNE-UP TIP: Remember, there are multiple steps to making the sale. You don't make it the first time you start to talk. There will be multiple steps. Each step needs to make it clearer and clearer how your business works until ultimately at some point you can say, "Let me tell you why you should want to become a customer."

That's how this system is designed to work:

1. You have a lead generation machine attracting your ideal customer.
2. You have a series of steps to educate your prospects and bring them closer and closer to becoming a customer. Each giving an idea, a wow, or some free value that makes them want to know more about your business. It's very common to have 4–5 steps.
3. You continue to follow a thoughtful step-by-step process until finally your prospects begin to ask questions about your business. This is the indicator they are "ready to buy."
4. You make your proposal or work up your quote and share it with your prospect who is now ready and very interested in doing business with you.
5. You set a timeframe to make a final decision so you can either get started or move on to your next prospect.
6. Lastly, you follow up to ensure your new customer received even better service than they were promised or they expected.

How do you do all this? Are you tuning in? Are you listening? Are you staying buoyant by educating prospects and giving away free advice or content?

Are you taking prospects through a step-by-step process that moves them closer and closer to the place they become a customer?

Make It Work For You

The vacuum we discussed is just a template that you can use however works best for you. Be very descriptive about what happens in each step of the process—all 8–12 steps or whatever you have. Remember:

1. Each step moves a prospect closer to becoming a customer by educating, WOWing and hooking them with free advice or content.
2. Not every customer needs every step. Some may take multiple steps at once.
3. Design each step in such a way that it will take even your most resistant prospect all the way up the ladder.

Keep this process in mind no matter what methodology you use. Before you pick one, however, let's discuss a few more key issues.

WHAT TO KEEP IN MIND WHEN CHOOSING YOUR METHODOLOGY

As I've said already, it's not important to use the methodologies I use as examples. All that's important is that you have *some* methodology that works the way you need it to.

I've found that *thinking in terms of a series of measurable and repeatable steps* helps to get an idea of how well folks are moving from one step in the process to another. If you do this, you can find out exactly where people fall off the ladder, so you know which step in the process needs to be fixed. So being able to measure each step is crucial, which means your process must be repeatable, so any problem can be identified and corrected.

As you put this together, there will be steps that you *think* are very important, but they will turn out not to be so important after all. Having a methodology that focuses on individual steps will make identifying any that are not as compelling as you might think easy to do. The goal here is giving you data, not a *gut feeling*, from which to make your decisions.

Once you find a methodology that works for you, you'll eventually be able to improve it or roll your own. That's what we're all about here—building a business with a solid enough sales vacuum that anyone can use it to convert a prospect into a customer. The only way to accomplish this is with a defined, repeatable process.

This will be extremely helpful for your sales team. It will let them know you want them to educate prospects first and then appropriately ask for the business through a series of steps that comfortably takes a person to the point where they say, "Wow, you are definitely who I want to do business with!"

This is a critical component on the front wheel of your bike, where the rubber meets the road. If your business is ever going to go anywhere, you need good traction in your ability to win new customers.

Chapter 24
MEASURING RESULTS

B efore we can sign off on the front wheel of your business, we must first spend a little time talking about a very important part of your process of winning customers, *measurements.*

There are many reasons why measuring results are important. To grow fast, you're going to need to be able to test and measure your efforts. The bigger you become and the faster your bike goes, the more important this becomes.

Each step of each process represents an opportunity for you to track activities and measure results. You must constantly ask yourself and team, "How is *this* going? How can we make it better?"

For some reason, many business owners don't do this. Frankly, I don't understand why because huge investments are made in this area. To be successful over the long term, you must have a process or methodology to determine whether an expenditure is wise or not. You'd certainly demand one when making a large investment in other areas of your business.

So the focus here is helping you establish good methods for measuring results in your efforts to win new customers.

CREATE YOUR FRONT WHEEL DASHBOARD

Remember that *dashboard*? We brought it up once before. Let's talk about it a bit more now. Below you'll find a very simple example of a dashboard built in Excel. I want you to notice how simple it is—*your dashboard doesn't have to be a complicated or costly software tool at all!* It's simply a standardized method for tracking and capturing data that can be represented graphically. Here, take a look:

Week Ending:	Metric #1	Metric #2	Metric #3	Metric #4	Metric #5	Metric #6	Metric #7	Metric #8
4-Jan								
11-Jan								
18-Jan								
25-Jan								
1-Feb								
8-Feb								
15-Feb								
22-Feb								
1-Mar								
8-Mar								
15-Mar								
22-Mar								
29-Mar								

You see? It's nothing more than a visual aid for making critical business decisions. It lets you quickly see what's going on under the hood of your business by visually showing you where you are making progress and where you are not.

A visual dashboard is the easiest way to quickly see patterns in your business. Without a dashboard for the front wheel of your bike, *you're at risk of spending dollars without return!* If your goal is to run a profitable business, you want to avoid this at all costs. Only spend money on your front wheel if it brings a return. To know if this is the case, *you need a dashboard.*

Track Your Results Weekly

For the best insights, your measurement timeframe should be *as short a period as you can reasonable measure.* For the front wheel, a good starting point is *weekly.* Don't wait to do this once a month. That's not enough. You need *at least* 52 opportunities to see the data, identify trends, and make adjustments. In fact, there may even be some activities that you want to track on a daily basis.

Measure Every Step

The final piece here is setting the goal to *measure each step of your process.* Some steps are more difficult to measure than others. You may want to measure only a few at first to slowly become familiar with the process of measuring and tracking since this will likely require a mindset change on your team to do regularly and consistently.

Start small and work your way up. As you do, keep in mind that *every step of the process is an opportunity to capture and translate activity into data, knowledge, and insight that will help you make better decisions.* I can't stress enough how important measuring everything is. You are making big dollar investments here, so make sure you measure the returns from your investment.

 TUNE UP TIP: Your Cost per Lead. The ultimate goal of measuring the performance of the front wheel of your business is fine tuning exactly *how much it costs you to generate a single prospect.* Not many business owners know how much each lead costs. Knowing this lets you calculate your cost per new customer, which lets you determine the return on investment (ROI) for your average customer. More to come on this later.

A STORY ON MEASURING RESULTS

One of my clients is a minor league sports team whose sales team consists largely of young college graduates interested in sports-related careers. By design, each year their sales team is different, with new graduates joining and experienced team members moving to other positions in sports management. The team's primary goal is selling premium tickets, sponsorships, game suites, etc., to local business owners who want to reach a large crowd of consumers interested in sports activities.

When these rookie salesmen and women arrive, they know little about selling or any sales process. So together we built a well-defined sales vacuum with specific processes for them to follow each step of the way. With the process, they are instructed to track and measure every activity that they complete. From making cold calls and attending networking events, to holding 1-2-1 meetings with prospects, they track and measure *EVERYTHING.*

As a result of years of tracking, the team now has a finely-tuned dashboard that shows them exactly what it costs to acquire a new customer. They have been able to translate that cost into the value of making each new prospect contact.

This means their new sales team members know when they arrive the value of making a phone call to a new prospect. They know with certainty how many phone calls it will take to get an appointment, how many appointments it will take to get a proposal, and how many proposals it will take to land a new customer. They also know the average value of a new customer package, so they can work the numbers backwards and determine the value of making a single phone call!

Knowing the value of each step of the sales process means they can translate that to their personal value outlined in their commission structure. The data from past years enables this. As you can see, measuring is not a burden, but a true motivator. What's more, they've done this with rookies instead of a high-paid team of sales experts. The results? As you might expect, they lead the league in sales performance every year. And you can do the same!

Take time before moving on to make sure you have solid measurement systems in place. This will be a powerful game-changer for your business.

SECTION FIVE

SERVING CUSTOMERS
OVERVIEW

Chapter 25

SERVING CUSTOMERS

No matter how good you are at winning new customers, if you can't meet the expectations you created on your front wheel, you'll never be able to keep them. As a business owner, you must find a way to ensure the *back wheel of your bike can keep up with the front.*

When you fail to serve your customers adequately, you'll have some serious problems in your business—this goes without saying. I understand this first hand because I saw what my father went through as he struggled with this aspect of his business.

Dad was natural at winning new customers. In fact, he was *so good*, that it was difficult to keep up with his ability to add new homes to our growing list of customers. Many of Dad's new customers came from referrals. On any given day, he'd get 3–4 new referrals (without even asking) from existing customers who would tell him about a neighbor who needed his help right away if possible.

Of course Dad would excitedly take the note, thank and assure them he would stop by or call right away, *and then proceed to lose the note somewhere in the van.* A month would go by and on the next visit, that same customer would ask why he hadn't called their neighbor yet. Dad would then explain how terribly busy he was and again promise to make it up to them. But in reality it usually took 2–3 reminders before he'd show up at that anxious neighbor's house.

As you might imagine, by that time the new prospect was no longer excited or interested. I am absolutely certain Dad's business would have been twice as large if he had simply followed a system or routine to follow up on new customer leads. Add to this my dad's inability to ever say "no" to anyone or anything, and you can see how his front and back wheels were running at two completely different speeds.

Dad's willingness to take on any job no matter how challenging often meant his business suffered because he could not keep up with the expectations he had set. Slowly but surely, this inconsistency started to wear on the patience and satisfaction of even his best customers. Eventually, Dad lost customers as fast as he gained them. In a way, Dad used his business more like an exercise bike— pedaling furiously but never getting anywhere.

I don't want you to only have one good wheel like my dad. You need a back wheel that can keep up with your front wheel so that you can keep customers coming back for more even as you continue to grow. To do this, we'll dig into the critical things you must do to ensure you over-deliver to your customers.

Chapter 26
DELIVERY STANDARDS

E veryone, including your prospects, knows it's *easy* to make promises about things you'll do in the future. However, it's quite different to fulfill those promises in a way that truly exceeds your customer's expectations.

Let's start with what's most important: *setting the standards for your execution or delivery.* An absolutely critical part of making your *delivery standards* work is being *crystal clear about your expectations.* You *must* tell your team very clearly what you demand and expect when engaging with your customers.

Many business owners ignore this. They allow their team to treat each customer like someone they meet on the street—doing *nothing* to make them feel *special.* The world is filled with businesses giving *average service* and never going out of their way. Frankly, that's a total waste. Why bother if you're not going to exceed expectations? I want something different for you. I want you to stand out from this crowd. To do that, you need delivery standards that are so high they put you above even your toughest competition.

You need standards *higher* than your stiffest competition, which means you need to research them. You need to go into your marketplace and *observe your competition at work.* The only way to truly understand their standards is to personally experience them. So buy their products, use their services, do whatever it is their customers do, and experience their standards. If you don't, how will you know where to set your own standards?

FIND OUT WHERE YOUR BAR SHOULD BE SET BY VISITING YOUR TOUGHEST COMPETITION

Become your toughest competitor's customer. See how well they communicate with you. Observe how well they deliver and if they meet delivery time frames. If they do, observe how they do that. Find out if you get *exactly* what you asked for or more. Take notes. *Write down important observations you have along the way before you forget them!*

You can do this with more than one business, but make sure to include your *strongest competitor*. You want the company that owns the lion's share of the market in your trading area. Use *that* business as your standard.

While researching, ask yourself, *how can we make ourselves unique from these guys?* Maybe there's an aspect of delivery they're falling short on. Every business has challenges and difficulties. If you can identify them, *you may just have found your competitive edge!*

If you find something, ask yourself, *could we do this better? If we really pushed ourselves, could we set a higher standard than this and consistently meet it?* Keep a list of anything you find yourself saying yes about. You'll *definitely* want to incorporate it into your delivery standards.

HOW HIGH STANDARDS SET YOU APART

Here's an example from my previous business where we manufactured doors. At the time, the industry standard turnaround time for orders was 3–4 weeks. A customer orders a product, and 3–4 weeks later it's been manufactured, shipped, and arrives on location.

So we asked the question, "What would it take to deliver any product with any configuration to any client within seven days?" By moving away from a 3–4 week turnaround to an unheard of seven-day delivery cycle, we knew we could truly set ourselves apart from the crowd.

So we put our heads together and asked all the necessary questions. And you know what? Slowly but surely we started making real progress. We didn't hit seven days immediately, but because of that goal, *we started to look at our entire business differently.* Shortly after starting the effort, we brought our delivery time down to just 2½ weeks. It wasn't too long before we hit 2 weeks, then 10 days. The closer we got, the more people noticed and *became excited about what we were doing.*

Our efforts were generating more and more excitement about what we were doing. People had started to notice we were *far exceeding* our competition. We were *WOWing* customers because we purposefully set our standards higher than our toughest competition.

You Have To Own This

You're going to need to find your own delivery standard, a place to put a stake in the ground and say, "This is what we're going to do and we're going to make this happen no matter what!" Wherever that is for you—make it your delivery standard.

You're the owner, so like everything else, only *you* can set the delivery standard expectation. I want to challenge you to *not be singularly focused on one aspect of your delivery to the point you ignore others.* That is, don't simply get good at one thing while remaining painfully deficient elsewhere. Apply your standard *equally across all aspects of your delivery system.* This is the only way to ensure your back wheel will keep up with your front wheel.

Even if know you can't reach your target in 12 months, set it anyway, tell your team about it, and share why it matters to your customers. Talk this through. Don't allow people to back off and say, "That's not possible." I've been through it and have helped client after client do it. *Everything can be improved.* It's simply a matter of putting enough effort and focus into it.

TUNE-UP TIP: Stay firm on your standards and don't settle! *Expect* your team to deliver the standard you set. *Expect* them to go above and beyond what's been the norm in your past. Have them take your customer's experience *to a totally new level.* Doing so will do *wonders* for your delivery process. Your customers will notice the change and they'll start telling others. Before you know it, you'll be the talk of the town—the talk of your industry!

LOOKING AHEAD

Make sure you are set on this stuff. Remember:

1. Research your toughest competition. Go experience their delivery standards.
2. Find specific areas where you could outperform them.
3. Develop delivery standards beyond your competition and tell your team about it.
4. Stay focused and don't allow your team to give up.

This is work, *yes!* But I assure you, if you do this, you'll have a solid back wheel on your bike. This will let you not only keep the promises you made on the front wheel, but *over-deliver* on them which will *WOW* your customers and keep them coming back for more!

Chapter 27

METHODOLOGY/
SECRET SAUCE

N ow that you've established your delivery standards, let's look at the next critical part of your back wheel: your *methodology* or *secret sauce*. I like this term because it puts the focus on how this part of your back wheel is *your business's secret to pulling off what others cannot replicate.*

Many businesses use their methodology to define what makes them one-of-a-kind. If you pay attention, you'll notice it everywhere, like Subway sandwich shops. When you walk into one of their shops, you can clearly see their secret sauce: a step-by-step process to build a sandwich in record time—*right in front of your eyes.* It's a quick, efficient, and fresh process that they developed to ensure they deliver each customer fresh food *made while they watch.*

How successful has this "secret sauce" been? Beyond Subway's clear success, their methodology has been adapted to several other food chains, for example, Chipotle. They just took what Subway was doing with sandwiches and did it to a burrito!

YOUR SECRET SAUCE

So what's your secret sauce? Here's an exercise to help you determine just that. Walk through this exercise with me:

133

1. Take out a clean sheet of paper or open a new document.
2. List 10 ways that you're **unique** from your competition.

What do I mean by unique? I mean list *any and everything* you do that you believe sets you apart from your competition. Write down whatever comes to mind. Don't justify or qualify it, just jot down answers to the question: *What is it that you offer that your competition does not?* You should be able to come up with a quick list of 10 things right away. Here are a few guidelines:

- Don't say things like, "We're focused on quality."
- Don't use generalities like, "We use the best products."
- Make it *specific:* what are 10 ways that your business *truly* operates uniquely?
- Focus on things that your customer would see or feel.

Once you have 10 unique items on your list, review it and ask two very specific questions of each item on the list:

- **Q1: *Can my competitor say the very same thing?*** If your competitor can say the same thing to anything on your list, then it's not unique. Scratch if off. You probably have 3–4 things on your list that must come off because your competitors can say the same thing. That's fine, scratch them off. What's left will be truly unique, that's what's important.
- **Q2: *Does my customer care?*** If something on your list doesn't really matter to your customer, strike it off. Ask this question and reflect on the answer from your customer's perspective.

Anything remaining on the list *must* pass these two criteria:

- Something that your competitor can't say, and
- Something that your customer genuinely cares about.

EVALUATING AND REBUILDING YOUR LIST

Here's an example to think about. As I went through this exercise with one client, one of the things they put on their list was, "We've been in business for 25 years."

The first answer was clearly, "No. My competitor cannot say this." So it passes the "unique" test, but then we asked, "Does my customer care?" The answer? "Not Really. They primarily care about a quality product and great service." So we took this item off their list.

You may strike everything off your list the first time, and that's okay! Just *think more deeply and come up with 10 more.* Repeat this process until you have a few things that pass the uniqueness and the customer care tests. Keep going until you've exhausted your list of ideas. In the end, you'll have a list of a few truly unique things that will be the essence of your secret sauce: *the things your customers love about what you do that no one else can replicate.*

BRANDING YOUR SECRET SAUCE

Once you've got the ingredients of your secret sauce, it's time to brand it. So the next thing to do is ask, "How do we brand this and make this methodology uniquely ours?"

Here's an example that might help: one of the sub shops near my office is called *Jersey Mike's.* Jersey Mike's essentially follows Subway's model, but with their own unique twist: you come in, there's a fresh selection, you call off the board, they slice the meat, they slice the cheese, they slice the bread, and they add all the spices, sauces and veggies to your liking.

Besides slicing your meat and cheese fresh when you order, they've also created a unique combination of spices, dressings and toppings to put on your sub that they call "Mike's Way." Now this simply means: you get lettuce, tomato, onion, salt & pepper, and oil & vinegar on your sub.

Notice that instead of listing a fairly simple combination of ingredients that make their subs taste unique, **they *branded* this methodology and called it *Mike's Way.*** Now, when you walk in to Jersey Mike's, you say, "I want a #7 and I'll have it Mike's Way." It's a way for them to package their uniqueness and differentiation while at the same time branding it.

Can you do this for your business? This is why you need to think through what makes you different, particularly from your toughest competitor: to make sure they can't copy your methodology. This may take some thoughtful wording to incorporate into your brand, but the payoff is your competition will not be able to say the same thing. As long as your customers truly care about your secret sauce, this will work.

Using Your Secret Sauce Moving Forward

Your secret sauce is a critical element of your business. With it, you can honestly tell your prospects, "We're the only place you can get this, because we're the only ones who do it!"

Make this one of your non-negotiables in your business, *one of those things that your team doesn't do just sometimes, but does all the time*. This must be applied across the board to everything you do. Everybody that joins your team, no matter what shift or location they are in, must serve your customers in your unique way because your methodology is your ***differentiator!***

Chapter 28
PROCESS FLOWCHARTS

O kay, now that your methodology is in place, we need to get into the mechanics of making sure your back wheel rotates well. Let's make sure you have good traction and a nice steady flow on the delivery side of your business. This all starts by making sure that you're working your business by *using process flowcharts.*

Using *processes,* rather than allowing everyone to use their own approach, is critical to the success of your delivery system. If you don't have processes, your critical activities are not *documented,* and you don't really own anything. If this is what you are doing, your customers are getting a wide variety of outcomes when doing business with you. Their experiences are hardly consistent and positive. They're not getting WOWed every time they transact business with you.

Your customers deserve better than that: they deserve the same credible, excellent service in the same reliable way no matter when they engage with you or no matter who serves them. Imagine you own a restaurant and every time I order chicken soup, it tastes different because every time I come in, a different cook makes it using their personal recipe. How could you hope to keep my business? It is not likely that you could.

You have to avoid this happening in your own business. This means you must have recipes or process flowcharts that control the back wheel of your bike. I've got a six-step method for putting process flowcharts in place in your business.

STEP ONE

So the first step is **build a checklist for critical processes in your business**. To do this, bring the people together who are directly involved in or have active daily engagement with whatever process you're working on. Ask them to simply write down a *step-by-step list of actions that happen* (from step 1 to the last step) whenever that process is done.

So if a customer submits an order, what happens? Write out a list, the simplest form of a process. If you only get that far, you'll be *way* ahead of most business owners who haven't even written any processes down. By writing this down, you create a virtual checklist that anyone could follow as they fulfill an order. It's as simple as can be, but you have to start somewhere.

STEP TWO

Next, **create a basic flowchart**. Now when I think about flowcharts, I use the very technical tool: *sticky notes*. Okay, I'm kidding about technical, but they *are* a great tool here. So this is no complex flowchart. *I'm literally using sticky notes.* Grab a few different colors of sticky notepads and you are ready to go- that's about as complicated as it needs to get!

See the image on the next page. A light-colored sticky note might mean that you're creating a document. A darker color, maybe blue or purple, might refer to data entry of some kind. Still another shade may be a handoff—moving from one person to another, or one function to another. You could use a color like green to represent when you're adding value, building the product, or delivering the service—making some contribution to the product. Red could indicate a hold or wait period, an opportunity.

So take your checklist and go into detail on each step. What is the activity and what color sticky note best represents it? Make sure you are clear about what actually happens at each step of the process. Your process is not likely to be linear. There may be different activities occurring simultaneously. If your process is making a product, step one is probably a customer placing an order, so use your receiving data color there. If you create an order form, use the color you use for document creation.

Next, if the order form goes into a system, use the appropriate color for the data entry step. Step three may be where the order gets handed off from the inside sales team to your manufacturing manager or shop guy. Use the color note that represents a handoff here, and so forth. Can you see how a series of activities is turning into a process flowchart? Simply follow the rest of the check list in detail creating sticky notes for each step in the appropriate color.

Now, take all those sticky notes and post them in sequence on a wall or large poster board. You are literally building the step-by-step sequence of activities that shows the flow of things happening in your business. Some activities may split off into multiple others, make sure your sticky notes accurately reflect this.

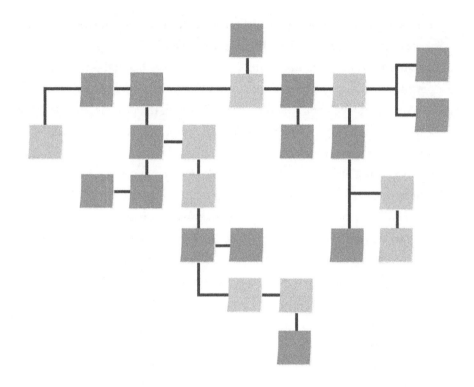

When you're done, you'll have a fairly clear picture of exactly what happens (see the image above). Next, draw in arrows that represent the direction of the flow. I use color-coded sticky notes because when your notes are arranged in their proper order, you can look at your flowchart and quickly see opportunities for improvement like where you have multiple handoffs or waiting periods.

A bonus-extra that comes from this exercise is becoming very aware that *the actual value add time of most processes is very minimal compared to the total process time*. If the total process takes 2 weeks, the value-add time may still only be one or two days. Experience has taught me this is often the case, which means there are major opportunities for improvement.

STEP THREE

Step three is simple: Once you have the chart laid out, look it over for ways to make improvements. Before it's a permanent document, take time to make it better. Remember to look at the different colors as they may represent your biggest opportunities for improvement:

- Look for hand-offs and ensure that these are being handled properly to prevent the ball from being dropped at these critical junctures.
- Look for wait or hold periods and see how you can improve or reduce them.

STEP FOUR

Next, transfer your colored sticky notes to a real document, your actual flowchart. There are several software tools you can use for this. Even Word and PowerPoint work great for process flowcharts. I strongly recommend creating a digital copy and storing it in your cloud so you can easily share it or make changes at any time.

STEP FIVE

Step Five is simple and very powerful. Once you've created your electronic document, **post it** where everybody on your team can see it. Put it where everyone can find it and make sure they know to follow it. This location may be on your website. It doesn't have to be a physical spot. Many of my clients use Google Drive, Trello, or Dropbox to maintain their process flowcharts. As always, find the one that works right for your business.

STEP SIX

Finally, train your entire team on your process flowchart. They need to not only know they exist, but also how to follow them. *So train everybody!* Once you have trained current team members, include the training in your new hire orientation process.

Some of these processes may be so critical to your business that you may decide to make reviewing and understanding them part of your new-hire proficiency tests. Make certain that new team members know you take this seriously and require them to demonstrate their willingness to follow them before you bring them on board.

Once new team members complete their orientation process, you now have a way to hold them accountable. Remember to build in measurement points and activity tracking so you can measure how well your team is doing at following your processes.

THE KEY TO SUCCESFUL PROCESS FLOWCHARTS

I believe the most important thing to retain here is that *everyone in your business must follow your process flowchart without exception.* You must follow them, your general manager must follow them—**everyone must follow the processes you create!**

With process flowcharts, your business will become very streamlined, and your products and services will experience high-quality, regular, and dependable output. This is also where you can make real profitability improvements: by streamlining your process flowcharts. This is a *powerful* way to improve the back wheel of your bike.

Chapter 29
SCRIPTS & TEMPLATES

Now, we need to make absolutely sure the back wheel of your bike is running just like a machine—doing the same things over and over again so that it becomes a *routine*. The goal is to have everything work like a Swiss watch. We do this with *scripts & templates*.

Scripts & Templates are very powerful tools that work hand-in-hand with the processes you just built to give you a superb back wheel on your bike. If you are turned off at the term *scripts* and are thinking about how they are contrived, insensitive, etc., I want to challenge your thinking.

WHAT SCRIPTS CAN DO FOR YOUR BUSINESS

Remember the last time you watched a really, *really* good movie? One that won an award for best picture? I can assure you this: *not one of those actors was just ad-libbing their lines. Each one was following a script.* Notice how there was nothing insensitive or contrived about their performances? The difference is that *the actors have practiced their script so often that they can deliver it in character in a genuine and believable manner.*

So scripts are only contrived when they are not rehearsed to the point that they are delivered like a character in a movie. Scripts are a great tool to help your team improve.

The goal of using a script is to help your team achieve proficiency. That's why they are important to your business: they allow you to develop a team proficient in the delivery and execution of your processes. Here are just a few positive things they do for your business:

- The simple act of writing out what needs to be said to your customer in the most positive and effective way adds clarity and certainty. As you see your written script, you'll identify gaps that need to be filled or phrases that need to be used (or avoided) to best deliver your message to your customer.
- There is power in getting your words correct and making sure they are delivered professionally, powerfully and positively. You can only get this with practice. Scripts let your team get the crucial practice they need.
- Having scripts helps your team develop a deeper understanding of your culture and unique positioning in the marketplace. No one should be allowed to go off script until they'd demonstrated proficiency with the script. Only then should they have the option to test new approaches with your customers.

Moving Beyond Scripts

How do you move your team beyond scripts? There may be situations where you NEVER want to deviate and still others where you decide your team has followed a script long enough to try changing a few things. Just make sure that whatever you change you can track and measure.

When you have sufficient results to demonstrate both proficiency and consistent results, then it may be time to allow some people on your team to add some of their own flavor to the message. Once you've developed team members, they can take you to another level at engaging with your customers in new and exciting ways. But only after you know that they have delivered consistent and proven results. The fundamental logic to this process is:

1. Get proven results first
2. Make modifications to get even better results.

It *must* be in that order. Do this with *every* routine communication you have with your customers. This includes dialogs on the phone with your prospects, inquiries you get in your customer service department, and initial conversations your technicians have at your customer's home. Write out the specific script of what you want them to say and how to say it. List the questions you want them to ask and the sequence of their responses to specific, routine questions. Use your known customer engagements and replicate them in scripted versions. You may even have multiple scripts depending upon the question asked or the situation encountered by your team.

I've had one specific client who has done this in extreme detail. They built a script for every possible issue a prospective customer could have. Once they had them all written, they put them into topics inside a large binder that is now a huge training tool for anyone who joins their team. They have a well-designed and well-articulated method so that anybody can step into any role and deliver exceptional service. Anyone can deal with almost any back wheel issue because it's all written out and prepared in the form of a script.

HOW TEMPLATES HELP YOUR BACK WHEEL

Besides scripts, templates help with other aspects of your back wheel processes. Here are two very critical reasons to use them:

Reason #1: They Keep You From Leaving Something Out

They help make sure that you don't inadvertently miss anything. For example, if you're asking questions of a customer on a call, templates are a quick and useful way to be able to make sure that nothing accidently gets missed.

I have a story to make this point clearer. Recently I scheduled to have a broken window replaced at my home. I placed the order and was told to expect installation in about a month.

The day of the scheduled installation, I took the morning off from work so I'd be there when the repairman showed up. However, when he arrived, the first thing he said was, "Geez! I didn't know that the window was on the second floor."

I responded, "Well, why didn't the scheduler ask me that when I made the appointment?" He didn't have the proper equipment for a second-story installation with him, so we had to reschedule the installation! *How crazy is that?* It cost the company lost time for their technician, fuel costs to drive to my home, and a future customer. I had just wasted half a day's work and now I had to go through the whole process a second time!

This all could have easily been fixed had the person who took the service call had a template outlining each and every question that should be asked to cover any potential situation. A quick question like, "Is the window on the first or second floor?" could have saved them a lot of trouble, costs, and a customer.

Reason #2: They Keep You From Making Errors

A template keeps people from making inadvertent mistakes. There's a Japanese term for it called "poka-yoke." Poka-yoke simply means "mistake-proofing." It's like a jig on a machine that keeps you from cutting raw material the wrong size. A template is a safety device preventing your staff from making mistakes.

There are several ways you can use templates to help with mistake-proofing the back wheel of your bike. Remember, mistakes on the back wheel mean you have expenditures where there should be profit. Look across all aspects of your delivery systems and consider how and where there are the opportunities to avoid mistakes. Where can you avoid errors of omission, of missing component parts, and of moving too quickly? Templates may be just the tool you need to bring discipline and consistency to your back wheel.

You Need Them Both

So there you have it—scripts & templates. You need them both! You've got to have those poka-yoke items, those templates. And if you're talking to people, talking to your customers, talking even between different operations in your business, then you've got to use scripts. Make sure that's where your team is starting. Once they've shown proficiency, then they can step out on their own, but not until then. It's too important to your customer.

Chapter 30

CONTINUOUS IMPROVEMENT

N ow I want to focus on a concept that I believe is going to be a real game-changer for your business. One that will let you truly set yourself apart from your competition in a way they'll never catch up with. How cool would that be?

What I'm talking about is applying *the methodology of continuous improvement* in your business. Continuous improvement means never being satisfied with where you are. Wherever you are today is okay. In fact, it may already be the best in your industry. But the question continuous improvement asks is, "What are you doing to consistently find ways to make it just a little bit better?"

The more you do this, the more you will continuously elevate your team's performance. This means your competitors *will never* catch you because they'll constantly be aiming for where you just *were* instead of where you are now. So even if they hit their aim—they're still behind!

Let's cover four things that will be very helpful in the area of continuous improvement.

STEP #1: FIND A METHODOLOGY

The first assignment is *find a methodology* that works best for you and for your business. There are many different continuous improvement templates, so before you begin, find the one that works well for your specific business type.

This may require some outside research on your part. One methodology for continuous improvement is called *Kaizen*, also known as the Toyota Production System. Its focus is on *rapid, continuous improvement.*

The approach entails assembling a small team of people who focus on and analyze a particular problem for a very short, defined period of time. They brainstorm, test, and then implement recommendations to improve the targeted process. In our workplace, we used the Kaizen methodology every week. We'd start on Monday and by Friday, we were celebrating our wins.

That's a methodology that worked for our business. But if you find one that works better for your business, that's great! Use it. Bottom line, you need one that you can articulate across your entire business to engage *everyone*. So start by finding the right methodology.

STEP #2: TRAIN YOUR TEAM

Next, *train everybody on you team* on the methodology you choose. Don't just train people in your shop, but train everyone. *Everyone* needs to be trained on your methodology.

Realize how big of a game changer this could be. It could truly make your business stand out and keep your competition from ever catching up. Everyone needs to know how you're going to continuously look at your business to make it better each week and month so that in a year you'll hardly look like the same company.

STEP #3: BUILD A SCHEDULE

Next, *build a schedule* for which processes you are going to work on and improve first. Look across your business and *start* with the places that are the highest opportunity for you. These will likely be the processes where you have the most invested or are most critical to the delivery of your product or service. Front wheel, back wheel, frame—it doesn't matter where you start. Pick the one that is *most important for you right now.*

Then, build a calendar for the year or at least for the next quarter. This will help you begin to *develop a rhythm* so that the people in your business always know on a regular basis, that things change and improve. This will help everyone get behind this, NOT as a *once-and-done* type program, but *instead* as something you're going to do over and over again until a habit and a rhythm develops and a true schedule of continuous improvement in your business emerges.

STEP #4: CELEBRATE THE WINS

Now the last step is really fairly simple but is often overlooked. Take time to *celebrate your business wins with your team.* That's right, *celebrate the wins!* Every time you complete your continuous improvement cycle, block out time to celebrate the achievement. It doesn't have to be game-changing. Celebrate *the small wins*—put them on your celebration calendar.

The Lawrence-of-Arabia Approach

Treat this as Lawrence of Arabia did with his army when faced with crossing what was believed to be an un-crossable desert. Lawrence of Arabia set a small goal every day and at the end of each day he took time to celebrate that day's win with his team. Then he would set a new goal for the following day and his army would focus only on that next day's goal. By doing this, they were successful each and every single day, and as a result, they soon found themselves having crossed the entire desert—a remarkable accomplishment.

This is how continuous improvement works in your business. You achieve small wins daily and weekly, and over time, you end up achieving a goal that you would have otherwise thought to be well out of reach.

CONTINUING TO IMPROVE

If you build this simple four-step process into your business there is no way your competition can keep up with you. I know because I've experienced it with my business. We stayed many steps ahead of where our competition thought we were. This made running the business fun and exciting because it didn't matter how much our competition knew or if we lost a person. No matter what was going on today, we were already working on the next big improvement.

I want for you to be bulletproof like that with your business. Put these things into place, then systematically make improvements throughout your entire business, and you will be!

Chapter 31

DELIVERY MEASUREMENT

Without measurement, it's impossible to know how well you are doing. This is truly essential to your business success. So let's dive into the final topic for this section: *measuring results.*

 TUNE-UP TIP: Every step of every process is a *potential opportunity* for you to measure. If you truly want to go as fast as possible, you need to measure, test, measure, test, measure, test...and move on. That's what allows you to *gain speed* in business. So really get it into your head that all processes everywhere are opportunities for you to measure the effectiveness of your efforts.

Here's a straight-forward 3-step process for measuring the results of your delivery efforts—the back wheel of your bike:

1. **Step One:** *Determine which results are the most critical to your business.* That is, the things that matter most in delivering timely, quality products to your customer.
2. **Step Two:** *Identify the industry standard for each process within your business that you are going to measure.* You need to know what's happening

in the marketplace. What are others doing in that particular quantifiable area of delivery? There's only one way to set your ultimate performance bar. *Start by understanding the industry standard.*

3. **Step Three:** *Build a dashboard.* Your dashboard will be the set of graphs that capture your progress in each area you have decided to measure. You can use it to see how you're trending—if you're moving in the right direction or not.

What you want is a delivery dashboard that measures the different things you want to accomplish in the delivery side of your business.

WHAT TO MEASURE ON YOUR DASHBOARD

Now you might be thinking, *okay, I get it, but what kinds of things should we measure?* Let me give you a couple of ideas to get you started:

1. If you're in the service business, consider *service response time.* For example, *how quickly are you getting to those calls that come in asking for service?* Measure this on a daily or weekly basis.

2. If you're in manufacturing or production, measure *production rates. How many of each product are you producing in a particular hour, day or week?*

3. You might consider *equipment up-time. Are your systems always available? If you're in the tech business or if you're providing IT, what's the up-time performance of your various systems that you're supporting?*

4. Perhaps you should measure your *failure rates.* How often are you making mistakes or getting something wrong?

5. For businesses with a physical product, you may get *returns*. *What do those returns look like? What causes a return? What opportunities can tracking this present?*

6. If you deal directly with customers, consider tracking your *complaints* or *inquiries*. Knowing these would give you data on which to make improvements.

This list is by no means comprehensive, rather, it's a start to get you thinking. You know your own business. Take time to review your own critical delivery processes and the items to track on your dashboard will become very apparent.

Don't leave the back wheel of your bike without first identifying what is most critical for you to measure. Take your time putting together your measurement for this. If you do, then your bike is going to go *really fast*.

If not, you're going to end up like my dad and lose customers as quickly as you win them. Don't let that happen to your business!

SECTION SIX

BUILDING A
WINNING TEAM

Chapter 32
BUILD A WINNING TEAM

Your team includes everyone who makes your products, delivers your services, and interacts with your customers. They do the work of peddling your bike so your business moves forward. For this to happen, it is important that you position your bike's seat in a way that allows them to put maximum power into the pedals.

Many successful business owners would tell you that success starts with your team. I agree. Without a strong team, you don't really have a business; you've got a J-O-B. Thinking about this brings to mind one story about how my dad violated one of the cardinal rules in business concerning your team: *never hire your relatives.*

Dad was all about hiring relatives. In fact, his business was built with the intention that his eight sons would be his first eight employees. But as it happens in so many businesses, when you hire relatives, you give up much of the needed objectivity and candid performance feedback your business needs.

Dad was no different in this regard. Over the years, had we not been his sons, we all would have been fired at least a few times—and for good reason. For not being ready when the normal workday begins, for talking back to our supervisor (Dad), for doing sloppy work, for taking too many breaks, and for not cleaning up after ourselves.

But Dad never seemed to mind. At least he didn't show it. Perhaps it was because he knew he couldn't find help that would work as cheaply as we would! Or maybe he felt guilty about taking away our weekends as teenagers to work 7am to 6pm while our friends loafed around at the pizza joint.

The results of these decisions on my dad's part, no matter the motivation, were that he set a very poor precedent in his business. When Dad started to hire team members who were not his own sons, he didn't have the discipline or expectations in place for them to follow. Without knowing it, he had undermined his own standards by allowing sub-par performance from his sons that made it impossible for the business to be successful without his being personally involved in every aspect of it. Not that we didn't work hard, because we did. But we also let our Dad carry the load *far too often*—something he was more than willing to do. No matter how much we loved one another or had good times together, *this is no recipe for success in today's business world.*

As a small business owner today, you must establish a sense of responsibility, accountability, and integrity on your team. You must lead them to ALWAYS serve the current customer well and pro-actively prepare for the next even before they arrive. This is the *only* way to sustainably grow a business in today's competitive market. Otherwise, the success of the business will fall entirely onto the back of the business owner—a heavy load no one can sustain for very long.

I know my dad tried. And he's one of the strongest guys I've ever known. But it still wore him down like it would any business owner, like it will you if we don't prepare properly. So that's what this section is about: building the kind of winning team that gives you the freedom to delegate responsibilities across every aspect of your business.

Chapter 33
CULTURE & NON-NEGOTIABLES

I f you've ever ridden a bike where the seat isn't adjusted properly, you know how uncomfortable that can be. The ride will be painful, it will hurt in ways that you can't explain, and you will not enjoy it at all. It's the same in business. If you don't setup your team correctly, they will not enjoy working for you. Our goal is to avoid this situation.

Do you struggle with keeping people motivated, having good employees leave, or your team becoming frustrated with the job and not enjoying coming to work? Maybe they've lost the passion and excitement they once had? If any of this sounds familiar, then you've got an adjustment issue with your seat. This doesn't mean your business is broken—it just means it needs a tune up, which is what this book is all about!

So where do you start? Start by setting your culture. That is: *define the things that you consider in your business to be non-negotiable.* Now, many people will tell you that you can't "define" culture—that it just happens and somehow evolves. I don't believe that for a second. Instead. I firmly believe that you, the business owner, must clearly and precisely define what your culture needs to be in order to best serve your customers.

TUNE-UP TIP: Think about any great company or organization. They all have a uniquely distinct culture, don't they? Do you really think that's by accident? *It's not.* It doesn't just occur from time to time for a lucky few companies. *Not at all.* Instead, these companies have created a successful culture by setting out to do just that in a very determined way.

The owners of the best businesses have built expectations that define their culture into the fabric of their business so they don't have to watch it daily or be available 24/7. If that's what you want for your business, then you've got to set those cultural expectations, you've got to set some non-negotiables as the foundation. That's why it's imperative we start here.

STEP *1*: SET YOUR NON-NEGOTIABLES

Now, like most things in this book, I don't want to overcomplicate this. Instead, I want to give you four very specific things to do that will help you build the culture you want in your business. So firstly, I want you to think about *6–8 things* that you consider to be *non-negotiable.*

Now the term *non-negotiable* is not something you hear that often, so it probably deserves some clarification as we get started. I use this term to mean something that is NOT an option in your mind. It's not up for debate. Consider it to be something that you are unwilling to allow in or around your business.

The non-negotiables for your business should fall into one of these three categories:

1. A behavior that *no matter what happens, you want it and you expect it to be done in your business.*
2. A behavior *that you won't tolerate at all in your business.*
3. A behavior *you know your customer will or should demand when doing business with you.*

So, when we talk about your non-negotiables, we're talking about things that fall into one of these categories. All businesses should cover at least these three categories when defining their ideal culture.

As you start out, it's probably going to be easier to think of *negative* non-negotiables because there are some things that you know you want to avoid. These "things I won't tolerate" items tend to be easier to define and articulate.

For example, you might initially say, "I want our phones answered by a person. I don't want our customers or prospects to talk to a voicemail box." Another example may be, "It's not okay to arrive for work late. You must be here on time. I expect you to be here before the office or store opens so that you can be prepared. When we open the doors for our customers, I want us all to look like we're on the job and ready to roll."

It's okay to start with negative items because these are often the issues you are dealing with most often day in and day out. Write down 6–8 specific things you want to be non-negotiable. Be real with yourself, the things on this list *must*:

1. **Be Personal:** They must mean something to you.
2. **Relate to your customer:** They must represent something your best customers would not tolerate either.

So that's your first step: get those 6–8 initial non-negotiables set.

STEP *2*: RESTATE YOUR NON-NEGOTIABLES POSITIVELY

Now, once we've got negative non-negotiables, we need to make them more appealing and palatable so your team can get behind them. To do this, your next step must be to *restate them as a positive*. Declaring 6–8 negative statements as your desired culture won't motivate anybody. So turning them into positive statements is a crucial step in the process.

Here's an example that might help: One of my past clients owned a hearing aid company. They helped individuals find hearing aids that suited their personal needs. As you might imagine, many of their clients were elderly and therefore needed significant assistance because of their poor hearing.

- **The Initial, Negative Non-Negotiable:** One of the things that the owner said that was a non-negotiable was that he didn't want anybody simply handing people off without helping them get from place to place.

He said it was not okay to just say, "See Sally three doors down on your left," or "I'm going to put you on hold then transfer you to Bob who will help you." He didn't want that type of customer interaction. That was his initial negative non-negotiable.

- **The Restated Positive Non-Negotiable:** When he restated his expectation, he said, "We will take our customers by the hand and walk them through each step of the process until they're completely satisfied and their order is fulfilled." Think about the visual picture of taking someone by the hand, reaching out and saying, "Ma'am, let me take you to the person who is going to help you," and then personally assisting them from place to place, and step to step.

Can you see how what started as a negative became a very clear, positive visual of the expectation? This can be a very powerful tool for your business. So what happened to this client? As soon as he published this non-negotiable and shared it with his team, they not only understood, but they could "visualize" it. This would have never happened if he had presented it in the initial, negative formation. This is now an integral part of their culture.

STEP *3*: DEFINE YOUR NON-NEGOTIABLES IN YOUR INDUSTRY "LINGO"

This step is powerful: *define your non-negotiables as something related to your industry.* In other words: *articulate the idea of your positive non-negotiable using words commonly used in your industry, trade, or specific business.*

Here's an example of a powerful way to connect with your people to make this happen. I work with a local non-profit organization that provides *equine therapy.* That is, they use horses to help with therapeutic healing. So, all of their culture statements (the positive version of their non-negotiables) are stated in terms related to horses.

They refer to being financially responsible as having a "solid footing" (which in a riding arena is the specially packed dirt that horses walk and run on). They also use the phrase "unbridled passion" to reflect the passion for and commitment to serving their customers inherent in their culture. By relating everything in their culture statements to their industry, *people in their industry "get it" because it speaks directly to what motivates them.*

Think this through for your own business. Trust me, this can be very powerful in defining the culture you need, want and expect.

STEP 4: HOLD PEOPLE ACCOUNTABLE

Once you've defined your expectations, you've got to be ready to hold your team members accountable. There must be a point at which you are prepared to ask someone to leave your team for failing to meet your non-negotiables. You must be prepared for them to exit your business and replace them with someone who is both willing and able to live within your desired culture.

If you tolerate people in your business who don't live up to the standards that you set and the culture that you want, *you're going to get exactly what you deserve.* If you have already allowed this to happen, you know the kind of damage and turmoil it can cause within your business. Others will question whether you are serious about your non-negotiables. Those who are detractors will enlist others to join them. It really only takes one bad apple in the bunch to spoil the culture for everyone. I'd suggest that fixing this doesn't start with the individuals on your team, *it starts with you, the business owner* making the commitment to hold these behaviors as non-negotiable.

SUCCEEDING WITH YOUR NON-NEGOTIABLES

Let's run down the major points of the chapter one final time to make sure we're on the same page:

1. Start by being crystal clear on what you want in the first place with your negatively-stated non-negotiables.
2. Restate these non-negotiables into positive statements of behavior that your people can visualize.
3. Take these positively-stated non-negotiables and restate them in terms or jargon related to your industry—using terms that everyone is familiar with.

4. Finally and most importantly, *hold your people accountable to your non-negotiables.*

Take time to figure this out. Do what you need to so that everybody in your business knows exactly the kind of culture you want and expect. When that happens, *people will come on board because they love the culture you're creating.* That's what it's all about, that's what I want for your business.

Chapter 34

THE HIRING PROCESS

Here's a different way of thinking about your hiring process: it's where you have the opportunity and obligation to protect those who earn the right to be on your team. This process is your first line of defense. During this process, you'll build a wall around your team that 1) sets them apart from those on the outside and 2) makes others *desire* to join your team.

I'm not a big fan of hiring just anyone, hoping it goes well, and then allowing them to wash out only to repeat the process all over again. That's a *very* expensive way to do things, your customers don't like it, and it discourages your other team members, creates bad vibes, and can corrupt every aspect of your business.

TUNE-UP TIP: It's in your best interest to make sure that it is **difficult** for people to get onto your team. Instead of taking anyone who applies, you want people to put in effort and earn the right to be on your team. This will help you weed out those who won't play by your rules once they are on your team. You've heard the adage, "Hire slow, fire fast." It is wise advice. T*ake your time in the hiring process. Make it deliberate. Make it purposeful. Make it difficult.*

Once you make a hiring decision, if that person doesn't live up to your non-negotiables, let them go quickly and repeat your entire hiring process with even more rigor. Whatever you do, *never* make your decision on a new hire quickly. If you do, you're only setting yourself up for disappointment. To ensure you don't, I have a somewhat lengthy 8.5 step hiring process I'd like to share with you.

STEP 1: CREATE A JOB POSTING

I strongly believe you should create your job postings based on *the behaviors you want*, not based on *the skills you need*. Both are important. But, if you find people with the right types of behaviors and attitudes, you can train the skills you need.

That's a general rule, so it may not hold perfectly true if you're hiring for a specific technical discipline or expertise. Businesses involved with specific technical expertise must test for the technical competence they need to execute the business. But, instead of being singularly focused on the technical skills, look for the behaviors you want. This will help you ensure you're considering people who possess both the skills *and* behaviors you need.

Here's a list of behaviors that you may consider adding to your job postings to get you started:

- 100% organized, structured, and disciplined
- Assertive, aggressive in a positive way, outgoing personality
- Strong communications skills, active listener, problem solver
- Leader, tireless energy, constantly looks for opportunities, takes the lead on new ideas
- Creative, good visual thinker, naturally aware of style, observant
- 24/7 Ambassador for the business
- Sales oriented, always looking for opportunities to engage with new prospects

STEP 2: SETUP A JOB HOTLINE

Next, I suggest you set up a *job hotline*. That's simply what it sounds like: a voicemail box job candidates can call in on to let you know that they're interested in applying for your open position.

In your job posting, ask people to call the job hotline. On the job line, they will hear a recorded greeting that prompts them to leave a message regarding their interest in the position. This is a great way to cast a wide net and get a large number of potential candidates for your open position.

Here are some pointers to help you with your hotline:

1. There are many services you can use. You may have an extra line on your existing phone system that you can dedicate for this purpose. If you need an extra line, a couple of low-cost options to consider are www. onebox.com or www.ureach.com. Both are web-based phone systems that allow you to set up a phone line dedicated to receiving voicemail messages.

2. Set up your phone line to use a "Custom Greeting." For your custom greeting, create a recording that welcomes the caller and gives them the instructions for how you want them to respond. To get you started, I've included a sample script you can adapt and use below:

    Thank you for calling the (Company Name) Job Candidate Hotline. (Company Name) is an award-winning technology and consulting firm specializing in helping associations make technology SIMPLE so they can focus on growing their organization.

    We're growing and current looking to add an (Position Title) to our team. The specific job responsibilities and skill requirements are listed in the job posting.

    Our ideal candidate is someone who will quickly become a key team member and someone who our clients and staff will rely on to deliver innovative and timely solutions. We are looking for someone who enjoys being self-managed, can thrive in a work-from-home environment and will become an integral part of a high-functioning team of technical specialists who all work from home.

    This is the first step of our application process. If you're interested in applying for this position, we've got three questions we'd like you to answer here on this voice mail message. You'll have 2 minutes to answer these questions. You may want to grab a pen and paper and write down these questions.

Here are your three questions:

- *Question #1: What relevant experience do you have which qualifies you for this position?*
- *Question #2: What interested you most in this opportunity?*
- *And Question #3: What unique skills and behaviors would you bring to our team?*

Please leave your Name, a Contact Phone Number and Contact E-mail and we will get back with you promptly if we are interested in having you take the next step of our application process.

Thanks again for calling the (Company Name) job candidate hotline.

DO NOT accept resumes or allow potential candidates to enter your hiring process without responding to your job candidate hotline.

STEP 3: GENERATE CANDIDATES FOR THE POSITION

With your job posting written and your hotline set up, you're ready to "fill the pipeline" with potential candidates.

Find 3 or 4 good web-based job posting sites where you can post your listing. Many small business owners use Craigslist as one source. It allows you to cast a wide net and it's not very expensive. You may also consider larger more focused sites such as Monster.com. There are also many smaller boutique sites like Indeed or Glassdoor that specialize in specific types of positions and locations.

To generate candidates, simply post your job listing in multiple places in order to *cast a wide net*. Make sure that each listing directs candidates to your job hotline.

STEP 4: SCREEN YOUR INCOMING CALLS

Now that you've got voicemail messages streaming into your job hotline number, you're ready to begin the initial screening process. This is where you will gain tremendous efficiencies. Just listen to each incoming voicemail message. It won't take longer than 1 or 2 minutes a piece. But in just a couple minutes each, you'll get a good sense of all potential candidates. Specifically, consider these questions:

1. **Did they follow the instructions they were given on the recording?** If they don't bother to leave a message or don't answer the questions asked, you've saved yourself 100% of the time you would have wasted on them—they would not be a good fit for your team.

2. **Can they clearly articulate who they are and why they're interested in your position?** As you listen to their response, consider whether they could communicate well with your customers. (How they answer any particular question is less important than whether they are articulate and would be capable of communicating with other team members and with your customers.)

3. **Did they follow the process steps?** If they don't follow your process steps during the hiring process, how likely is it that they're going to follow your processes when they're in your business, especially when you're not there? It's not very likely they would!

So as you listen to each call and consider these three questions for each, flag or note those who are most impressive so you can invite them to the next step of your hiring process.

STEP 5: CONDUCT A GROUP INTERVIEW

Once you've selected the best candidates from your job hotline, it's time to schedule and conduct a *group interview*. This might sound a bit odd or intimidating, but let me encourage you to give this a try.

Interviewing is a game. Some people are very good at the game and in a one-on-one interview, they can and will *"game"* you. They know how to behave and what to say during the one-hour interview. These gamers can be very impressive, like an actor in a play.

However, when you put *all* candidates into a group setting at once and take them through a structured group interview, you put them in a situation that is difficult for them to control. Instead of seeing their formal, prepared persona, you will see their normal behavior. During this process you will see each person's true character.

By placing all of your top candidates into a group setting, the top two or three candidates are going to shine immediately. Within 10 minutes, you'll know far more about who you want to move forward with than you would from taking a week or two to do indvidual interviews.

Here is a recommended agenda for your group interview:

1. **Company and Position Overview:** Spend 10–15 minutes giving an overview of the company—your history, why you got into the business, what sets you apart from your competition, your culture, and where you're going. Also give an overview of the position—the responsibilities, how it fits into the organization, the growth opportunities, the compensation structure, etc. Be transparent!

2. **Ask the Candidates Questions:** Spend the next 30–45 minutes asking questions of the candidates. Let them know that everyone will be asked the same question. Start with one person and go around the table. For the next question, start with a different person. Rotate who goes first. (The key here is to watch for body language, posture, expression, etc., as much as the specific answers. Keep an eye on what those who are not answering at the moment are doing. It won't take long to determine which are best suited to "fit" into your organization, regardless of skill). Here are some examples of questions that you might ask:

   a. "Describe for me the most complicated and difficult customer situation you have had and what made it so difficult."

   b. "Tell me about a situation where you felt that your customer was making a bad decision and you helped them make a better one. How did you do it?"

   c. "If you had the opportunity to either work solo or with a large team of people, which would you prefer and why?" Etc.

3. **Allow the Candidates to Ask Questions of You/Your Team:** Turn the tables and invite the candidates to ask any questions they have of you and your team members who are present. Stay as long as there are questions. Be candid and honest with all answers. Your goal is for

them to leave with a very clear picture of the company, the people, and the position.

4. **Share Next Steps:** Explain to the candidates how the rest of the process will go—when they will hear back from you, what's next in the hiring process, etc.

5. **Say Goodbyes.**

6. **De-Brief with your team members:** Plan for your team to stay a while after the session ends. Use this time to review, critique and make decisions on who to move to the next step of the hiring process. You may want to hand out group-interview rating forms to candidates to elicit feedback about your process.

7. **Select the Top 2–3 Candidates:** narrow your list of top candidates to the top 2–3 and proceed to the next step.

STEP 6: PERFORM INDIVIDUAL ASSESSMENTS

Once you have your top 2–3 candidates from your group interview session, you'll need to perform *Individual assessments*. Use a structured assessment tool, not something superficial that simply interprets personality. Find an assessment tool that will really give you insight into that person's motivation, skills, tendencies, whether they like autonomy, if they like to work as a team, and so forth.

You may have an assessment instrument you're familiar with or already use. I prefer a comprehensive tool like ProfilesXT. A good resource for using this particular toolset is www.people-right.com. The folks at People-Right are very knowledgeable and can help you interpret the results to ensure you're making good hiring decisions.

These assessments are not very expensive, $200–$300 at most, and it's money well spent. You only need to use it on the few top candidates out of your group interview. Doing this will help you make sure you've selected the right person for the open, critical position in your business.

STEP 7: PERFORM ONE-ON-ONE INTERVIEWS

Finally you are ready to do *individual interviews*. It's important you don't do this until you're seven steps into the process. By now, people have had to earn their way to spend time with you because your time is valuable. *You should only spend time with those very best candidates.* Those who followed the process, performed well on the group interview, and scored well on your assessments relative to what you need for the position.

Then *and only then* should you spend time face-to-face with them in an interview setting. Here you can focus on the experiences, skills, desires, and aspirations of the individual top candidates.

STEP 8: MAKE THE JOB OFFER

Job offers come in all shapes and sizes. I won't go into detail here, but I do recommend you *WOW* your job candidate and make the offer *a very formal one.* I would also recommend you have it reviewed by your legal counsel prior to use. You may find they have some specific changes based on your industry, company location, etc.

Also, consider making your job offer *contingent on demonstrated job skills.* It is not unreasonable to ask a job candidate to "ride with" one of your techs or "spend time" with one of your team members before you make a formal commitment for full time employment. If you choose to do this, check with your legal counsel before implementing these or any other types of skill-based conditional factors.

But the bottom line is it's always in your best interest to make sure you have someone who *can and will* demonstrate their competency BEFORE you put them on your payroll.

STEP 8.5: USE AN ONBOARDING PROCESS

I call this Step 8.5 because this is really a bonus step. But it's important enough to spend some time on it. The idea is to *have a formal onboarding process* for all new team members.

If you have new team members joining your business and they walk in on day one and all you say is, "There is your desk and phone. Your coworkers will tell you how things work around here," and walk off expecting them to do what you need, that's just not enough. *You need to spend time with them.* Spend at least half a day with every new person that joins your business team.

What should you do with them? *Tell them your story!* Tell them why this business is important to you, why being successful in your business matters so much to you. Give them an idea of your vision for the company. Tell them what the non-negotiables are and why they are important to your customers. Get them excited about being there and tell them how important it is to you that they're on your team. *Spend time with them.*

Don't worry about repeating some of the things you shared during the hiring process. Repetition is good. They were very nervous during the hiring process and didn't catch much of it anyway. Repeat it again and again.

This will solidify their position in the business. Start with you and then have them spend time with the different functions in your business so that they can see how things actually work, how activities and functions fit together so that no matter what their position is, they begin to understand what goes on in other parts of the business.

CLOSING THOUGHTS

Here are two closing thoughts before we move on:

1. **Never settle:** Don't allow yourself to do it. Don't allow the desperation of adding someone to your team to shortcut the hiring process. No matter if it's a relative, a friend of a friend, or someone you've known for a long time—*take them through the process.* This process is probably the most important one in your business.
2. **Always be hiring; always be looking for great talent:** Set up your job hotline and just leave it up and active. From time to time, put a posting up that declares, "We're always looking for good people to join the team." Then keep your eyes open for strong candidates. Think of baseball—professional teams are constantly recruiting. They've got people looking for talent to join their team all year long.

Remember: *always hire the best people.* I can't stress enough how vitally important this is to your business. You have to spend time on this because it is essential you get this right.

Chapter 35

COMPENSATION STRUCTURE

N ow let's talk about one of the riskiest tasks you have when it comes to adjusting the seat on your bike. Your compensation structure is a powerful way to make the seat more comfortable so that your people want to get on and pedal hard for your business—but it is also very easy to screw up.

It is very important that you build a *compensation structure* that works—one that motivates and incentivizes your people in the proper way. It must also be consistent with your culture and the way you want your business to operate.

Many business owners get this wrong because they *jump to conclusions*. They look at what's going on around them without thinking about the implications. But I want something better for you, so it is important to take this slowly and deliberately. One thing is certain—this topic will impact your culture. *How you pay and incentivize your people and the structure you use to compensate them **will** impact your culture.*

BUILDING A COMPENSATION STRUCTURE TO MATCH YOUR CUTLURE
As we begin, I want to recommend a book called *Drive* by Daniel Pink. If you've not read it, there's a 20-minute YouTube video that outlines the essence of what

he found in his research regarding incentives and what motivates behavior. You'll want to become familiar with his research because you cannot motivate all the behaviors you want with compensation alone.

Many business owners put too much emphasis on compensation and fail to pay adequate attention to the other things that matter—like (1) having a clear and compelling purpose that people get passionate about and (2) allowing team members to master their own trade.

Here are five key concerns you must consider when developing your compensation structure:

1. Your Culture
2. Your Compensation Elements
3. Defining Your Spot on the *Risk vs Security* Scale
4. Determining Competitive Total Compensation
5. Determining the Job's Performance Standards

#1: YOUR CULTURE

The first thing to consider is, *what kind of culture do I want to create?* Consider the extremes:

- **Team Based Culture**: On one end of the spectrum is a completely team-based culture—no one wins unless everyone wins. The success of the business is driven by the team working together to score a victory. An example of this would be a NASCAR Pit Crew. On this team, *everyone* must perform their job well in order for the team to win. There's no chance for an individual to win—it's a complete *team* sport.

- **Individual Based Culture:** On the other end of the spectrum is a completely individual-oriented culture. Here, each individual is responsible for their own success. Internal competition is big as individuals vie for the top spot on the leader board. There can be big winners and big losers. A good example here is a commission-based car dealership or multi-level marketing business. These are largely *individual* sports.

Your business likely falls somewhere in between the extremes of being completely team-oriented and completely individual-oriented. So your culture needs to have the right balance of team-oriented *and* individual-oriented rewards that fit your business's specific needs. Your first consideration when building your compensation structure should be always keep your desired culture in the forefront of your thinking.

#2: YOUR COMPENSATION ELEMENTS

Secondly, consider the elements of compensation you want to have as part of your total compensation package. In other words, before you lay out your structure, think through the specific ways you plan to reward and incentivize people. Where and how will you allocate your budget on different forms of compensation?

Here are a few compensation elements you may want to consider:

- **Base Wage:** You will likely have people earning a base wage that may be tied to current market ranges and trends.
- **Commission Plan:** You may want some or all of your team to be able to earn commissions based on actual sales levels or targets.
- **Bonus Program:** You may decide that you'd rather use a bonus program for some or all of your team so that the rewards of your success are determined independently from any specific measure or metric.
- **401K Program:** You may want to support or fund a contribution to a retirement plan for your team members.
- **Allowances:** You may choose to pay for certain "perks" such as a car, phone, entertainment, etc.
- **Profit Sharing:** You may want to include a structured profit sharing program as part of your package to truly separate your business from your competition.

Lay out the different ways that you want to compensate your team. Make sure you identify all elements that are important or essential to your business so you can build a comprehensive package. Avoid thinking narrowly about a specific element or two. Instead lay them all out so you can get the big picture of what you want this compensation structure to look like.

#3: DEFINE YOUR SPOT ON THE RISK VS. SECURITY SCALE

Your next action is to define where you're comfortable being on what I'll call the *risk versus security scale.* For example, imagine that you're selling insurance or own a car dealership. You may be comfortable with 100% of each person's compensation being based on how well they do in terms of sales. Perhaps you feel more of an obligation to pay at least a small base wage that is supported by a commission structure allowing each person to achieve a nice total compensation based on their sales results.

Some business owners run their business so that they have a *very* small base pay, so most of the compensation is at risk. Others prefer to pay all their people a market-based base wage and offer a bonus that is not directly tied to business results. Neither is objectively right or wrong. It is simply a matter of business owner preference.

Do what is best for you as the business owner and don't be pushed into the corner by what others do. Consider it, reflect on it, then make the decision that best supports your level of comfort on the scale and is consistent with your desired culture. Those who are aligned with you and your culture will be drawn to your business no matter what.

#4: DETERMINING COMPETITIVE TOTAL COMPENSATION

Now look at the market and find out the competitive total compensation for every position in your company. Do this for every position: administrative assistants, production workers, engineers, drafters, sales people, manufacturing managers—*everyone*. You need to know the market compensation for every position on your team.

Once you know market compensation levels, you can break that target amount down into the different elements that you want to see as part of your compensation program. This will allow you to define your position on the risk/security scale so you can build your overall compensation package.

TUNE-UP TIP: When you do your market research on competitive total compensation, don't do it on your own. Don't just go to your friend who has a business and ask what he's paying. He may not know anything more about the market than you do. The best potential employees will know the market, so to attract them, you will need to perform your due diligence. Simply do a Google search and you'll find compensation data for most standard positions. There are many sources available to you, so keep looking until you find the right tool for you.

#5: DETERMINING PERFORMANCE EXPECTATIONS

The final concern is to determine the performance expectations for each position. This is something that can take several different formats.

For example, if you are working on a sales position, such standards or expectations might be stated in terms of an *average sales amount*, or perhaps it would include a *monthly revenue generated* target. Each position is going to have different expectations that tie directly to what you need and expect from that position on a routine basis (weekly, monthly, etc., depending on the position and your business).

For a few more examples, if you are working on a position in production, your expectation here would likely be related to productivity. Additionally, you'll likely want to define a safety metric or target. If you have someone in a professional role, you may use a billable hours or % of billable time measure as their performance expectation. Hopefully you can see how this process works.

So as you start to think about your comp structure, *think about these five concerns.* If you have taken these into consideration, you can be confident about your compensation structure because you'll be compensating your team members at or above the market average.

FINAL THOUGHTS ON COMPENSATION

One final thought: no matter what you do, very specifically and deliberately communicate your compensation methodology to your team. Don't do this in the dark and then hope that everybody understands. Instead, be very transparent. Share with your team your logic and your reasoning:

- Show them what you looked at when you determined the structure.
- Explain to them why it's important.
- Walk them through the elements you considered.
- Show them where you want to be on the risk scale.
- Let them see where the market is at.
- Explain your expectations to them.
- Break it down in terms of what this means to you to ensure they understand how and why this affects them.

When your team understands all this, they *get* your compensations structure. They realize that you have risk in this as well. Think about your culture. Be transparent about how your structure relates to it to ensure you people understand your thought process and don't assume you are making decisions flippantly. Explain this thoroughly and your team will appreciate it.

Chapter 36

TEAM ENGAGEMENT

Team engagement is all about getting everyone on your team 100% engaged in your business. By *engaged,* we don't mean just showing up and doing their job. We mean truly wanting to participate in helping make your business better every day. That's what it's all about.

The goal here is 100% engagement, *not 100% attendance or 100% acceptance,* but **100% engagement**. You don't want people that just check out at the end of the day not thinking about your business until the next morning. You should want and expect something better: team members who can't wait to share their ideas on how to make your customer's experience better, how to make your products more reliable, or even how to improve your services.

As the business owner, you must have the mindset that everyone in your business is valuable. It doesn't matter whether someone is the rainmaker bringing in new business, on the shipping dock sending out product, or at the reception desk answering the phone—they are all important. So it starts with you showing your team that you truly believe *everyone has a meaningful role* in your business.

How do you do that? To start, you simply *cannot* play favorites. In fact, I'll plead with you, beg with you even: *don't get caught in that trap!* It's an easy trap to fall into because people naturally gravitate towards those they get along with and are comfortable with. But as a business owner, you send a bad message to your team if you do this. They don't understand why one person gets attention and they don't. Instead, they see you playing favorites—*a huge roadblock* to achieving 100% engagement.

So no matter who they are: a superstar or someone struggling, *they're equally important to you.* You must spend your time with people at both ends of the spectrum—with the folks who are doing the menial tasks as well as those who are designing the critical elements of your business system. It doesn't matter what they do, show them that *everyone has a meaningful role in your business.*

Let's cover four steps you can take to boost team engagement.

STEP #1: FIND WAYS FOR EVERYONE IN YOUR BUSINESS TO WIN

The first step to building 100% team engagement is to *find a way for everyone in your business to win.* Now, you may be thinking, *Okay, so what does, "everybody win" mean?*

Let me explain by sharing a story from when I ran a manufacturing business. We had well over 200 people manufacturing a hard goods products. In the beginning, the people on the team were not very engaged in the business. They came to work and simply put in their time to get their paycheck. Their passion was outside of work (family, fishing, sports, etc.). They were not motivated to be at work—they did it only because they had to. They genuinely couldn't care less about what actually happened while they were at work. So my job was to find a way for everyone to get engaged.

So we sat down and defined what we wanted to happen in the business, the critical success factors that we wanted to achieve. We came up with five—five different areas that were critical to our success and then asked how we could improve them. Once that was set, we brought everyone together for an all-hands-on-deck meeting. I shared with them this message:

> "Here's the deal. We have defined five areas that we must become very good at and we have set goals for each of these five areas. If we hit our goals in all five areas, and I am confident we can, then I'm going to give my personal Jeep to one of you! I'll put all of your

names in a hat, mix them up, pull out a winner, and that winner will drive home in my Jeep."

You can imagine the response. People started raising their hand asking questions about how many miles the Jeep had on it, if it had air conditioning, what sort of interior it had, etc., so I answered. As they became more interested in their opportunity to win my Jeep (and take advantage of the boss!) I said, "I'm going to drive the Jeep until we hit these five goals. But I am confident you can do it. So there's the challenge for you. Win and you can 'stick it to the boss' because *I'll literally give one of you my Jeep!*"

Immediately after the meeting, several people went outside to see my Jeep, and I know they were thinking, *Wow! Okay. This is a pretty nice Jeep. This is worth it.* Over the next several months, people would come up to me and say, "Hey, how's my Jeep?" And I'd respond by reminding them that I was going to continue to drive it until we hit all five of the goals we had established for the business.

Fast forward five months, we hit all five goals. We were rocking as a business, and *everyone was 100% engaged!* They found ways to engage in the business because they *wanted to win.* I shared our results with the team and told them we were having a celebration party. I took the Jeep to have it detailed so it would look brand new. We rented a local performance hall for the night of the big celebration and arranged a big dinner party for all team members and their families. Then we rolled the shiny, polished Jeep right on to the ballroom floor!

When it came time to give away the Jeep, we took our time with the drawing to make it fun for everyone. Eventually my Jeep went to a 28-year employee in the maintenance department. I signed the title over that evening and he drove my Jeep home. I finished the night by telling my team, "I now know that you can do anything you put your mind to." And from that point on, we did. *The business flourished as a result because everybody was engaged.* My ride home that night wasn't all that fun, because I rode with my wife who thought I had just lost my mind!

Am I recommending you give away your car? *Absolutely not.* But what I'm telling you is *be creative and think of ways for everybody to win.* For another example: I had a client recently use a group trip to Hawaii to boost engagement. He set the bar pretty high, and soon after he shared the challenge with his team, all the walls and windows in his office were covered with charts showing what needed to happen to accomplish their goal. They hit their goal for the trip one month before the deadline—*and everyone packed their suitcases for Hawaii!*

What can you do to find a way for your team to win? It can really transform your team from one where everyone just shows up to work to one where everyone is **100% engaged** in your business.

STEP #2: CREATE WORK TEAMS WITHIN YOUR BUSINESS

The next step to achieving 100% team engagement is *find a way to create work teams within your business.* Instead of assigning different functions to individuals, assign them to work teams. For example, everyone in a single office could be a team, so they could have some team assignments, achieve team recognition, and be given team incentives.

Do the same thing for your people in production and for those who work in the field or remotely. Create a team around them because team members will lift one another up. They'll help each other. They'll get together on a regular basis and if anyone is having a rough time, someone on the team will step in and lift them up. If someone is holding them back, their teammates will step up and motivate them. You won't have to do it yourself.

I can tell you, creating work teams is powerful. You don't have to have a hundred people in your business to do it. Even if you only have six or eight employees, create two teams. There could be a little friendly competition if that's consistent with your culture. Or you could simply have a way for them to measure team performance so you can see how they get better.

 TUNE-UP TIP: Here's a good one: I've got a plumbing client who put their plumbers into separate teams. As a result, the members of each team **cross-train one another** to boost the team's productivity as a whole! By putting people on a team, they naturally want to improve when compared to their peers. A mindset of *if these guys can do it, we can too* starts to develop. As a result, the whole business is lifted!

STEP #3: GIVE YOUR EMPLOYEES THE FREEDOM TO FAIL

Next, you must ensure that you've setup your business in a way that *gives your team members the authority and the freedom to fail.* Make sure that everyone knows it's okay in your business to try something and get it wrong.

This is going to require you to put some systems into place so that you can learn from and correct these failures when they happen. But whatever you do, avoid what I see so often: *when a failure happens, immediately, there's a punishment.* That's **not** the way to boost team engagement. What do you think that says to everybody else on the team? *Don't take risks!* Rather than setting them free like eagles soaring to do incredible things, you've clipped their wings. Now, like ducks, they'll be content to stay safe in the water where there is no risk.

What you want is for your team to take measured risks. Not foolish risks, but *educated risks* that let you help them learn as they go. In the end, this is the only way you're going to see who's capable of making the breakthroughs you need in your business. So put these two simple actions in place:

1. Give your people the freedom to fail without fear of punishment.
2. Find a structured way to learn from those failures and teach the rest of the team while praising everybody for having had the courage to take the necessary risks.

STEP #4: USE TEAM ENGAGEMENT TO IDENTIFY FUTURE LEADERS

Finally, use team engagement as a way to identify your future leaders. Your leaders will come from the opportunities you give your team. What happens is this: when you create a way for everyone to win, certain team members emerge as those that are going to organize other team members' actions to make sure the business does win. *These people* are your potential future leaders.

Additionally, when you group people into teams, natural leaders will emerge. You don't have to identify who the leader is, it will become very apparent. Groups will select their own leader, and those leaders will lift up their team. This is a great way for you to watch how people deal with small team leadership roles. Those who take smart and calculated risks and that learn from their failures are the ones you want leading your business in the future.

Team engagement is essential. It's how you build a team that can handle running your business even when you are not there. That's the goal here. To get that, you have to create the right kind of environment. You have to make sure that you've engineered it into the way your seat is positioned.

Brainstorm ideas that will get your team engaged. Use the ones here, or adapt them if you think they will work for you, but don't hesitate to do some research and take some time to think about this. Team engagement is key to keeping your business running as it should even when you aren't there. Picture that!

Chapter 37

PERFORMANCE FEEDBACK

Let's talk about your performance feedback system. Being able to easily and effectively give everyone in your business performance feedback is key to building a winning team.

This is a topic many business owners avoid. Perhaps they feel like they do it *on the fly*. Maybe they think a pat on the back is enough. Whatever the reason is, far too many business owners don't formalize their performance feedback or make it part of the structure of their business. This is a huge mistake. Don't miss this big opportunity to do something that will help you build a winning team. And don't think I'm advocating a complicated system or long forms to fill out— not at all! No, what I want for you is *a simple way to give performance feedback*.

Since we were kids we have all craved for performance feedback. Think about it. When you were in kindergarten, didn't you love getting a gold star on your work or having it put up on the board? You did. I did. *We all did*. It started back then and it still holds true no matter how old we get: people all want and need feedback.

You owe it to your team to give them that feedback. So you've got to find a method that will allow you to do this every 3–6 months. Waiting to do it on a yearly basis is too long. People need and want feedback more often than that. So let's consider a fairly simple method to accomplish this.

A SIMPLE METHODOLOGY FOR FEEDBACK

Here's a method I have been using that was adopted from General Electric (GE). Their tool for performance feedback was powerful. I've used it in my previous business and now, many of my clients use it as well. It's that powerful, and it works. Furthermore, it's simple and easy to apply.

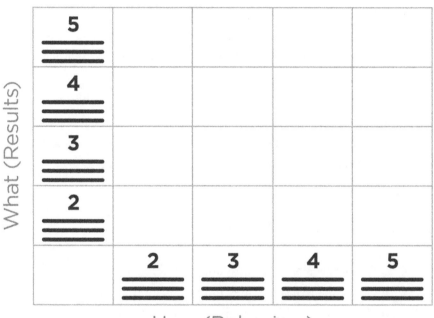

This matrix allows us to identify and classify two dimensions of performance:

- **The X-axis:** *measures what your team member gets done.* That's the first dimension of our performance matrix.
- **The Y-axis:** *measures how your team member gets work done.* This is the second dimension of our performance matrix.

Along both the X axis and the Y axis is a scale. The scale goes from 2–5, with 5 being the best and 2 being the worst.

The entirety of the performance feedback matrix I recommend simply encompasses two dimensions of performance: (1) *what they do,* and (2) *how they do it.* That's it. It's truly that simple.

Once you understand how the matrix works, next you can define what each rating on the matrix represents. This needs to be done for both the X- and Y-axis. Define what each number on your feedback scale represents:

- Each number needs to have a different set of criteria, so write them at the same time and compare them to ensure they are well-defined and distinct from one another.
- On the vertical axis, for each number write out a specific description of what the "what/results" look like in terms of a 2, 3, 4, and 5.
- On the horizontal axis, do the very same thing for the description of what your "how/behaviors" look like at a 2, 3, 4, and 5.

For example, considering the *how/behaviors*, you may want to describe how easy a person is to work with. Your ratings from 2 -5 might be:

- **2:** Doesn't get along well with others on the team
- **3:** Gets along well sometimes, but is difficult from time to time
- **4:** Normally gets along well, but does not go above and beyond
- **5:** Goes out of their way to help others be successful. Other team members love working with them.
- When it comes to the *what,* your scale might look something like this:
- **2:** Doesn't achieve performance standards very often
- **3:** Achieves performance standards occasionally
- **4:** Normally achieves performance standards
- **5:** Continually achieves and exceeds performance standards

Your definitions might read differently depending on your business. Don't be cryptic. Use detailed examples. You want individuals on your team to be able to visualize the words you use to describe each rating. The more detail, the better.

HOW THE MATRIX WORKS

Once you have your matrix setup, it's fairly easy to share this chart with anyone in your business and have them see two things fairly quickly:

1. **Expected Performance:** By designating a specific square on the matrix *where you want them to be*, you can quickly communicate both behavior (how) and performance (what) standards for your team.
2. **Current Performance:** Just as you can identify "expected" performance, you can identify "current" performance. A good way to do this is to ask each team member to rate themselves. Once they select the box that best describes their results and their behaviors, you can share with them where you rate them. This will allow you to easily have a conversation about the difference between the two perspectives.

This matrix can be used as a shorthand to tell your team members, "If your desire is to be here, *here's what that looks like.* I need to see the behaviors and results outlined on the matrix for that position." It gives them a clear goal or path to improve their performance.

Now let's add one more feature to this performance feedback matrix: *your bonus structure:*

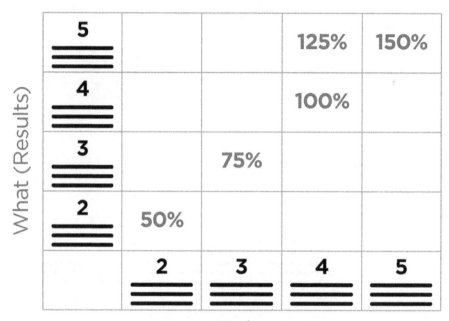

Now here I've added some % scores to the matrix. In square (2,2), it's 50% based upon performance, while on (5,5) the score is 150%. You see, this performance matrix also helps you communicate your **bonus structure** and how it relates to actual performance. *With these percentages, you can link individual performance to your bonus plans.* This way, bonus plan payouts (if you incorporate one into your compensation structure) relate directly to each individual's performance feedback.

The percentage designations in each box make it easy for team members to see the connection between the percentage of available bonus pool they earn and how they were rated on their most recent performance assessment. Those rated at the box with "100%" would get 100% of what was allocated for them. Those rated at "125%" would be eligible for 125%, those rated at "50%" would only be eligible for 50%, and so forth.

The percentages you use **don't** have to follow these numbers. You can go as low as 0% or as high as you'd like. Do whatever is reasonable for your business. The point is that employees quickly and easily see how the bonus structure links and aligns with individual performance. This will allow your people to become very focused on and motivated to make improvements.

USING YOUR MATRIX TO BECOME A PERFORMANCE-BASED COMPANY

What you'll find when you start using this matrix to do these things is that *it will transform your company into a performance-based company.* Here's just one example to help you see how this works:

I had a client who had no performance feedback system in place before we introduced the matrix. Over the first year, we simply familiarized the team with the matrix and let them become accustomed to how they were scoring on it. Then, in year two, we introduced the percentages and linked it into a bonus payout. All of a sudden, everything became *real* for the people on their team.

They suddenly realized, *Wow! I'm leaving money on the table. If I were performing at this higher level, I could get more bonus!* That lead them to taking very seriously where they currently rated on the performance matrix. It highly motivated them to figure out what they needed to do to get to where they wanted to be. The introduction of the performance matrix created significant positive change in my client's business.

I want the same for you, so here's your assignment:

1. **Create Your Own Matrix:** I've given you the start of one and all you need to know to edit and modify it to fit your business. It won't be hard to set it up for your needs. You may have already done this in your notes as you're reading through.

2. **Document Your Feedback Process:** Make sure to document how the process of giving performance feedback using your matrix works so that you can get into the rhythm of giving out feedback on a regular basis.

3. **Repeat This Feedback Process Every 6 Months:** This is not something that you will do once and then forget about. This is something you want to establish a regular 6-month rhythm on. Waiting a year is too long. Do whatever you can to do this at least every 6-months.

When it comes time to go live, introduce the process first as a measurement of performance. I want you to follow my client's example and just get your people adjusted to thinking in terms of the matrix. Then, when they are used to it, link it to your bonus plans.

That's all there is to it! Do these things and you will become a performance-based company. That's right, *performance based not seniority or position based.* You want proven contributions, results, attributes and behaviors that are consistent with your desired culture to be what drives your company forward.

This is important because it can really change how your people behave, which is exactly what you want. *You want performers.* Additionally, you'll have an easy way to tell underperformers that there are consequences to poor performance.

Chapter 38

RECOGNITION
& CELEBRATION

T his is our final adjustment to the seat your team will be sitting on as they drive your business forward. If we can get this right, your business will run without you there or having to worry about it. Then, you can sit back and simply enjoy the hard work you've put into your business. The last piece in this process is for you to *establish your recognition and celebration programs.*

Do you recognize performance and celebrate wins? You need to, because it's a big deal. We tend to get so focused on the day-to-day details of our business that often times we overlook the victories. When we look ahead at the next issue without taking time to appreciate the small victories, our team suffers. It's important to find a way for your team to sit back and revel in each small victory for a few minutes.

Make celebrating wins a critical ingredient in your culture. I hear many business owners say they want to have fun in their business. Yes, business should be fun. And by fun, I mean, you get to recognize the good things that happen and celebrate them with your team. That's the culture you want to have in your business.

TUNE-UP TIP: Don't wait for the big win. Don't wait for that time when you land that elephant client, when you close that big deal, when you finally make it big. Those moments come too infrequently. What's more, oftentimes, once they come, you're already onto worrying about other things. If you're waiting for the big win, you tend to miss all the little wins.

STEP ONE: CELEBRATE THE SMALL WINS

When I say celebrate the small wins, I want you to apply the *"Lawrence of Arabia* Approach". As we discussed earlier, Lawrence of Arabia was the leader of an army who famously took his army across a desert to attack an enemy city. Remember, Lawrence of Arabia didn't focus his army (his team) on crossing the entire desert. Instead, he focused and motivated his team to achieve a small goal each and every day.

Each day, he celebrated the victory of that day and set small, reasonable targets for the next day. Before they knew it, they had crossed the entire desert and were looking up at the city. This is how I want you to approach your business when it comes to celebrating and recognizing the victories. The first thing is *celebrate the small wins.* Don't wait for the big ones. Get in the mode and mindset where every single small victory is worth celebrating.

Your celebration doesn't have to be anything extravagant or expensive. It simply means that you're not going to wait for the big victory. Instead, you'll be celebrating all along the way. When you look for them, there are a lot of small wins to keep people motivated, excited about being on the team, and moving forward. Take time out to cheer, recognize and break loose a little. Have some fun along the way celebrating the small wins.

STEP TWO: FIND YOUR UNIQUE MOMENTS OF TRUTH

Next, *find your unique moments of truth.* A moment of truth is when someone on your team does something that's unexpected, something that's not part of their normal job and provides a benefit to another teammate, customer or supplier. That's the moment of truth. They see an opportunity and even though they don't have to, *they take it.*

The reason it's called a "moment of truth" is because in such a moment, that team member could have done one of two things:

1. They could take the approach that says, "That's not my job. I'm not responsible for that. That's someone else's." Or,
2. They could step up and go out of their way to make something happen. These are *moments of truth.*

Find a little trinket—a pen, a pin, a hat, something like that. It could be anything small, maybe a t-shirt, but *something that is unique to your business that you award to people who demonstrate behaviors and actions that you would call moments of truth.*

Here's an example of what happens when you do this: One of my clients uses a small pennant or flag. They're big into baseball and so they used a pennant with their logo on it. Whenever someone demonstrates a moment of truth, they are recognized by the team in front of their peers and are awarded a pennant.

When you look around their office, in their open cubicle/workspace area, you see these pennants flying everywhere. Some people have accumulated three or four pennants. It's just a small recognition. It doesn't cost much at all, but it recognizes those individuals who have gone out of their way to make something good happen for a customer, a teammate, a supplier, or someone significant to the business.

Instead of catching people doing things wrong, **try catching them doing things right** and celebrate that with them and the rest of your team.

STEP THREE: BUILD A CELEBRATION CALENDAR

Step three is to make planning ahead for the celebrations in your future a part of your culture. Always be anticipating celebrations. For example, if you have some upcoming milestone dates for your business that are worth celebrating, get those on a calendar and plan a celebration for them. Then let your team know about it and watch how they behave.

There are other things where you may not know all the details, but if you've got a big project, plan ahead for the celebration that's going to occur at the end.

Create that expectation that after a project *you will have a celebration* and just watch what happens.

STEP FOUR: LET YOUR TEAM OWN IT

The last step here is the most fun and rewarding. Be bold and *let your team own your celebrations.* Seriously! Let them own it. Once you've put in place the mindset that you're going to celebrate small wins, find a way to identify your unique moment of truth, built your celebration calendar, and then let your team of people pull it all together for you.

Remember, we talked earlier about finding ways to build work teams? Here's another opportunity for a work team. Pull 4–5 people together and make them responsible. Assign them as your celebration team. Then make it their job to work the calendar, to plan ahead, to go out and figure out all the logistics, and own your celebrations. Then all that's left is for you to sit back and enjoy your hard work paying off!

SECTION SEVEN

YOUR CUSTOMERS

Chapter 39

ENGAGING WITH
YOUR CUSTOMERS

I n this section we'll be talking about your customers, or as I like to think of them, *your race fans*. Let me ask you, have you ever been to a road rally or run a 5K race? Have you ever been in a situation where you must put out your best effort while people cheer you on and are excited by watching you perform your best? If not, I can assure you there's nothing more exhilarating than putting your best effort into something and having people around you truly appreciate your hard work and dedication.

That's the ultimate goal for your business and this particular section: *to surround your business with wildly loyal fans who become your unpaid sales people.* These people want to see you win because they're excited for you and believe in what you do.

But here's the sad reality: most customers leave the businesses they favor not because of bad service, but because of *perceived indifference*. The real reason most customers quit buying from one business and try another is because *they don't get a sense that the people in that business really care whether they stay or not.* It's a sad truth—one you may have even experienced in your own business.

So the goal of this section is to share some ideas on how to avoid and turn situations like this around so that your customers not only know you care, but are excited about what you do.

THE VALUE OF "SHOWING YOUR CUSTOMERS SOME LOVE"

I can honestly say my dad LOVED his customers and they LOVED him in return.

You see, there's nothing more important than letting your customers know how much you appreciate them and "showing them some love." This was natural for my dad. It wasn't contrived or fabricated. He genuinely cared about his customers.

In fact I can remember many occasions where after a job, Dad would go to the door with the bill in hand and would talk with his customer for what seemed like an hour. I'm sure it was only 10–15 minutes, but no matter what, he would talk, listen, laugh, and engage with each and every person he did business with. To Dad, there was no clock or tact time requirement. The relationship was far too important for any of that.

It was not uncommon for the post-job conversation to lead to other things that the customer needed to get done, and more times than not, Dad would motion for us to bring a ladder and come solve a problem for the customer. We might spend another half hour cleaning a chandelier, mounting a very high picture, or fixing a leaking downspout. And when we would finally get in the van to leave, Dad would admit he didn't charge them for the extra effort, but rather, he knew that the customer would "take care of him" the next time we came back. And they always would.

So let's spend some time going into detail about what it means to create raving race fans. Dad did it as part of his natural approach to his business. Let's make this natural for you as well.

Chapter 40
CUSTOMER FEEDBACK

Yes, your team is important. They are a very powerful and important group of people that we focused on in the last section. In business, however, no one's ever more important than the customer. To succeed, you've got to have a large group of enthusiastic customers or race fans that are going to help you grow your business in ways that just aren't possible without them.

Why do I keep referring to them as your *racing fans?* Remember the example of running a race I mentioned earlier? I'm sure you've been to some event where you witnessed firsthand how much the fans add to the atmosphere. Think of "home field advantage." How much harder is achieving victory without fans cheering your efforts? *In business, like in any competition, having loyal fans can be game changing.*

Business gets tiring, old, and frustrating when you don't get the sense that anyone cares whether you win or lose. That's why you need to put a high priority on your customers, so they will become your raving fans and keep you motivated to win and succeed.

KNOWING WHAT YOUR UNPAID SALES FORCE REALLY THINKS

I want you to see your race fans as your *unpaid sales force*. Imagine your customers helping you find new business and telling your story in ways that you never could, with credibility that you could never have. Imagine the benefits of having other people talking about you to your ideal prospects in a very positive way. That's what can happen when you establish ways for your customers to give you feedback.

Now you might be thinking, "I hate getting feedback surveys from people that I do business with. I never respond to their surveys. They send me these long, boring, useless mailings I just throw in the trash. I don't have time for it!"

Think about it this way: how well do you understand how your customers feel about your business? If you're like many business owners, you really have little idea how your customers truly feel about you and your business. Why? Because I spend a lot of time talking to the customers of my business owner clients. When I have those conversations, they often share things with me that they would not share with the business owner themselves. They don't want to be offensive, and they're willing in many cases to simply just put up with whatever they find lacking or frustrating.

But I don't want that for you. I want you to really know what your customers think. I want you to be crystal clear on how people feel about you, your business, your team, your processes, and whether or not they get the same quality of service or product every time they visit your establishment and engage with your team. I want you to know this with absolute certainty.

#1: FIND A METHOD THAT WORKS FOR YOU

The first priority in creating a customer feedback system is to *find a method that works for you*. There are many options to consider. You need to find the one that fits your personality and your business model. If you're not a fan of using SurveyMonkey or a similar surveying tool, *then don't do it!* If you're not a fan of making regular phone calls to your customers to ask for their feedback, *then don't use that method!* But you do have to pick one. *You can't rule them all out,* so focus on finding one that works for you.

Simply go to Google and do a search for "customer feedback systems." You'll find many different approaches. Most have been tested and validated. Some are intricate and sophisticated, others are very simple. No complicated system is needed here. You simply need a system that will allow you to connect with your customers on a regular basis and ask them to take a few minutes to give you some feedback.

I like to use SurveyMonkey. It's easy to build simple questionnaires that you can quickly send to your customers, and it is easy for them to respond. But you may find one that's different and better for you. If so, great!

Don't use the excuse none are right for you, ultimately *just pick one*. Frankly, it doesn't even matter if they respond. Here's the beauty of it: since many customers leave because of perceived indifference, all you have to do to get a leg up on your competition is to show that you *are* interested. Just sending the form shows a *perceived interest* from you that they feel that influences how they think about your service and your product.

So start by finding the right method. That's your first step. Don't overcomplicate it or make it overbearing. Just find one that you can get behind.

#2: ESTABLISH A RHYTHM

Now that you have selected a method for getting feedback, simply *establish a steady rhythm*. Just like we talked about in giving your team members feedback in a rhythm, you want to touch base with your customers with a usual rhythm as well.

I don't want you to be like many business owners who read a book or watch a video and then go out and create and send a very detailed and elaborate survey to all their customers only to never to be heard from again. They do it one time, think they learned something or just checked the box, then they go back to business as usual.

Instead, consider taking your customer list and dividing it into small groups. Then, every week, month, every two weeks—whatever rhythm you decide upon, send one group a feedback questionnaire. It can be once a quarter if that works for your business. Establish the timing, get into the rhythm, and create a habit of always sending a questionnaire to one group of customers.

You may review the last three months and identify which customers you've done business with. You may use an algorithm to figure out which customers you want to get feedback from. Simply establish your selection methodology. Then each quarter, use that selection methodology and send surveys to the group you define. The important thing is that you continue until you get into a rhythm. It's not overbearing for your team, and it's not a one-time overwhelming project.

 TUNE-UP TIP: What's the ideal rhythm? Start by shooting for at least once a quarter. Once a year is too infrequent to develop a rhythm. You don't get enough feedback to be able to make any adjustments in the course of a year. Without frequency, your customers have long ago begun to think you really don't care, so find a good, frequent rhythm (no less than four times a year) that fits your business.

#3: GATHER QUANTIFIABLE DATA

Whatever method you find, whatever frequency you use—*find a way to quantify the feedback results you receive into a visual graph.*

How? You could ask a simple question, like "Rate the quality of our service on a scale of 1–10, with 10 being outstanding and 1 being 'we suck.'" The results from that question are quantifiable and would work in a visual graph.

Be sure to make this part of your rhythm: every time you get your quantifiable data from customers, take the number, do the math, come up with an average, and chart it each time you do a round of surveys. Do that for all 3–4 questions you ask.

You will also want to get some more descriptive feedback in addition to the ratings, so make sure to ask a couple of open-ended questions. What's most important is that (1) you are interested enough to ask and that (2) you track the results so that you can measure feedback over time. Where you start doesn't matter. All that truly matters is incremental progress, so get that quantifiable data so you can track and know you are making that progress.

Looking at customer feedback data is as important as looking at your financials. Both are indications of how well your business is doing. Your financial numbers give you one perspective, your customers will give you another. Please don't miss the opportunity to get their perspective on your business. Remember:

1. Find the method that works for you.
2. Get into a rhythm. Do this repeatedly and in small manageable chunks.
3. Find a way to *make it quantifiable.*

If you do these three things with customer feedback, you'll be on the way to making a real difference in your business because your customers will *know* you care. This will solve the #1 issue causing them to leave.

Chapter 41

RELATIONSHIP STANDARDS

Now let's focus on setting relationship standards with your raving race fans, your unpaid sales force. Because you're the owner, you set the standards across your business. This is still true when it comes to how you interact and treat your customers. You alone have primary responsibility for setting the standards of your relationship with your customers.

Start by asking yourself some important questions:

- What am I going to expect from my customers?
- What am I going to demand of my customers?
- How do I want my team to work with my customers?
- How do I want them to behave when engaging with my customers?

There is no right or wrong answer to these questions. There's only what you decide. The important thing is that you do NOT leave this to the individual interpretation of different team members in your business—that's like having no standard at all.

WHO REALLY OWNS YOUR RELATIONSHIP WITH YOUR CUSTOMERS?

Let me share a story about who really owns your relationship with your customer. I was with someone recently who had just gotten a new job for a lumber yard here in Texas. The construction trade is booming right now, so that industry is strong.

I was interested in his new job, so I just asked him how he got it. He told me, "The guy that I'm replacing left and he took all of his customers with him. Which worked out great for me because they were really hurting and ended up making me a big offer to bring my customers with me."

So who is really winning on this deal? Are these businesses getting better or are their customers really "owned" by the sales person? You don't want this to happen in your business. *You* want to own the customer relationship, not your sales team. If you expect this to happen, you're going to have to be the one setting the customer relationship standards your team follows. To help you set these standards, I have five key points I want you to consider.

KEY #1: CREATE RAVING FANS

The first thing you want to do in your relationship with your customers is *create raving fans.* You've heard the term raving fans before. Many people use it. If by chance you haven't, raving fans are the people that are more than just okay with what you do—*they love what you do.* In fact, they're so passionate about what you do and how you do it, they tell everyone they know about you. They're just wildly excited about having done business with you. So the first thing you need to know is *how to create raving fans.*

Start by having a discussion with your team. Decide what specifically you are going to do to go above and beyond your customer's expectation. Decide what you are going to do to "blow them away" and turn them into raving fans.

This needs to be a specific, deliberate discussion with your team that lasts until you come to an agreement. Your goal is to get to a place where everyone says, "Yes, this is what we're going to do, and this is how we're going to do to it. We're going to do it the same way every time, so we make sure that it happens to every customer, all the time."

Recently, I did an online transaction with a business representative. I didn't think much about it. I bought a neat product from them, and then I thought the deal was over. But shortly after I finished the transaction, I got an email from this representative and he said, "Hey, just thought I'd ask, what size t-shirt do you wear? We've got a t-shirt that we would like to send you as our gift for being a great customer."

I didn't expect the t-shirt, nor was it something I needed. I've got plenty of t-shirts in my closet, but I told him what size I wore, and sure enough, three days later, a small package with a really cool t-shirt from this company arrived along with a simple note that said, "Hey, thanks for being a great customer!" They blew me away! Guess what? I'm talking about it right here—see how it works? So sit down and figure out with your team what you can do to create your raving fans.

KEY #2: ESTABLISH EXPECTATIONS FOR INTERACTING WITH CUSTOMERS

Next, establish the expectations that you have with your customers. That is, establish the way you want your team to engage with them. I call these your *engagement expectations*. If you want to stay connected with your customers on a regular basis, then it will be important for someone on your team to follow up with them every 30–60 days if you've not seen or heard from them. Establish the expectation for connecting with your customers on a regular basis.

Build this into your program. Build it into the position agreements you use with your folks who engage with customers. Make sure that they know what your expectations are. Many sales people simply deal with whomever they are speaking to without doing any follow up or outreach. They make no attempt to connect with customers who they haven't seen in 3, 4, or 5 months. Almost any customer would enjoy a call where the only purpose was to say, "Hey, we're just thinking about you!"

I was speaking recently with a business owner about this. She is a special lady with a very unique voice. As soon as you hear her voice on the phone, you know it is her. She recognized the importance of regular communications with her customers, so she set a standard of calling every customer that she hadn't seen in over three months. Each new month she gets a report of her last three months of customer purchases and then compares that list with her overall customer list. When she finds a customer who has not made a purchase in the last three months, she gets on the phone and simply says,

> *"This is Christy. I just wanted to let you know I was thinking about you. I hope you're enjoying the drapes you bought in August. We miss you and would love to see you back in the store. Come see us when you get a chance. We'd just like to get up to date on how things are going. I hope you and your family are doing well."*

And sure enough, this simple message brings people back into the showroom. Since implementing this standard, her business has grown faster than ever because she has a standard and expectation for customer communications.

KEY #3: GET PERSONAL WITH YOUR CUSTOMERS

Is it time to *get personal* with your customers? Find a way of getting personal with your customers that works for you. You may not be a touchy-feely kind of person. In your personal life, you may be a little bit detached or introverted. I get it. That's fine. I'm not suggesting you give your customers a big hug, send their kids birthday cards or whatever.

But ask yourself: *Do your customers really know your team? Do they know you? Do they feel like they matter to you, or do they think of themselves as just another transaction to you?* Get personal! Find the level of personal engagement *that works for you.*

For example, maybe you do an outing every now and then, bring them together in a group, or have some social activity to participate in. Find that extra way to engage them that fits your personal style. It's okay to spend some time making sure you get this one just right.

KEY #4: BE HONEST & CANDID WITH YOUR CUSTOMERS

This is a no-brainer—be honest and candid with your customers. If something goes wrong, accept responsibility for it. If you know something isn't right or that your product or service is not a good match for them, *let them know*. If it's clear that they're not doing their part of the transaction, call them on it just like they would call you on it.

Honest and candid engagements with your customers build trust and mutual respect. People prefer to do business with those they know, like and trust. Trust must be there. It's a critical piece. So find a way to be honest and candid.

There's another side of honesty: accepting it when you hear it. When you get feedback that isn't necessarily 100% positive, you've got to ask, "What can we do to get better? Thanks for that feedback. We needed that kick in the behind to get us back on course. We promise to do better. No excuses. This is on us. We're going to own this." Now this goes for more than just you. Everyone on your team needs to adopt this attitude. So set the standard, and make sure your team follows through.

KEY #5: GRADE YOUR CUSTOMERS

This can really be a game-changer for you: *take time to grade your customers A, B, C and D.* You've heard this before, but let me break down what each grade should represent:

- **A Customers:** These are awesome customers. Your raving fans, your ambassadors—the ones out there promoting you more than your sales team.
- **B Customers:** B Customers are solid. They pay on time, they do good repeat business, they're likable, they're enjoyable to do business with, and you love them.
- **C Customers:** These customers cause you and your team some challenge. They may be difficult to work with, require special hand-holding, or are slow to make decisions. They may come with some baggage. Often times they are slow to pay their invoices.
- **D Customers:** These customers are the ones who every time they come in, your whole team looks the other way hoping somebody else will take care of them. When your team sees their caller ID, they say, "Oh, not again!" They are more difficult to please than it is worth. They do

not respect you or your team members (you know you have them, everybody does).

Grade your customers first and foremost so you can fire your D Customers. Quit spending time on those customers that bring you down, that don't live up to their part of the deal. You've got a standard for your team and for your business. Don't let the bad customers pull you below the line. Don't let them burn all your resources. Make sure that you've got time to focus on your A and B customers. Here's what to tell them based on the grade:

- **Tell your A Customers**: "We love you!" Involve them in your business. Get personal with them. Make sure you're creating raving fans here by going above and beyond.
- **Tell your B Customers**: "Look, you're a solid customer. We'd love for you to be an 'A' customer. Here's what that looks like," and then show them what your A Customer looks like.
- **Tell your C Customers:** "I love having you as a customer, but I need you to step up and become an A or B Customer in order for us to continue to do business with you."
- **Tell your D Customers:** "We're no longer going to do business with you for these reasons. Here are some recommendations of other businesses you may want to check out. Good luck. Bye"

I can tell you story after story about people who have done this and it's been game-changing. I know it's fearful to tell customers to go packing. People don't like to do it. But it's in your best interest, so spend some time thinking about how you can get rid of your D Customers.

So follow these five keys: (1) create raving fans, (2) establish expectations, (3) get personal with your customers, (4) be honest with them, and finally, (5) grade your customers and *fire those Ds!* I know you can do it, and you'll be glad you did!

Chapter 42

CUSTOMER APPRECIATION

A nother key with your customers, your race fans, is making sure they know without a doubt that you appreciate them. This must be a conscious effort on your part, something you plan throughout the year and build into everything you do in your business. This may mean setting aside a budget, scheduling time, or coordinating events in order to show your customers you truly appreciate them.

This is not something that requires a lot of money or time. There are many large companies that do this well without spending a lot of money on it. A great example is one of my wife's favorites, *Nordstrom's*. Now, if you've ever been in a Nordstrom's, you know it's not the most inexpensive store in the mall. In fact, it's fairly upscale and prices are set accordingly.

But it doesn't matter whether she buys a $4 pair of slippers or a nice formal dress, inevitably, two or three days later she receives a handwritten note in the mail from the sales person thanking her for the purchase! The card reads:

"Ms. Allen, thanks for stopping in. It was great to see you. If you have any questions, don't hesitate to call. Let me know the next time you're coming, I'd love to see you. We'll help you out with anything else you need."

A personal handwritten note on a card that probably cost $1.50 total. That's practically nothing! But they do it for the big purchases *and* the small ones. They don't spend a lot of money, but my wife *knows* they love her. Now *that's* appreciation.

See my point—*it doesn't have to be grand*, even if your business is upscale. This isn't about spending money, it's about letting your customers know you *genuinely* appreciate them. To help, I want to spend the rest of the chapter on three ideas that will take your customer appreciation game to the next level.

IDEA #1: FIND A WAY TO MAKE THEM FEEL SPECIAL

Start by *finding a way to make your customers feel special.* Do this one as a team; pull everyone together and discuss this. Get them thinking creatively and "outside of the box." Brainstorm things that would make your customers truly feel appreciated.

Brainstorm. No idea is a bad idea. They don't need to be about your industry or related to your business or your product. Don't assume the only way to show appreciation is through typical things—like logo gear or a useful trinket. Instead, brainstorm ideas that might be a bit odd or unusual.

Be creative. Send them a gift card, invite them to an event, or even give them a special offer to another local business. You may find this even helps build your relationship with that business. In some cases, other businesses may even pay for you to use their products or services as a way to show your customers appreciation because of the exposure.

There are hundreds of ways to do this that don't cost much but will show your customers you're looking out for their best interest. So find a way to make them feel special. Then, don't just do it once, but do it again and again. Find your rhythm. It may be once a quarter or twice a year, but *do it.* You don't have to tell them if or when something special is coming—just surprise them and show them they are special to you.

IDEA #2: CREATE A CLIENT REWARDS PROGRAM

Secondly, *create a client rewards program.* The idea here is to create a way for your clients to get something from you for continuing to do business with you over time.

Again, no need to make this big, expensive, or overly significant. You don't even need to promote this. Consider making it a "bonus extra" they get for being a regular or repeat customer. It could be as easy as simply promoting customers who reach a certain threshold on your social media page—there's no need to overthink it.

Here's an example: I work with a sports marketing company that works for a local sports team. When their customers purchase sponsorships, season tickets, executive suites and related items, they have 8–10 specific "bonus extras" they give them all season long. After signing up, customers begin receiving these bonuses including invitations, offers, and various other perks. Every two weeks or so, a new one arrives. They keep their list of bonuses creative to ensure customers are excited about them and also take the opportunity to stay in constant communication with them.

As a premium customer of theirs, I get invited to special events or activities each month. I know these offers don't cost them a lot, but they think it through and continue to regularly express how special I am to them. Can you do the same for your best customers?

IDEA #3: SURPRISE & INSPIRE YOUR CUSTOMERS

Another way to show customers appreciation is to *surprise and inspire them.* Give them a surprise gift. Recall the t-shirt I mentioned earlier? That was a token of appreciation, and frankly, I loved it! I didn't need it, but it was awesome because *it was a surprise.*

Here's another example to consider: one of my clients is a florist who focuses on high-end, distinctive floral arrangements for weddings. They are among the best in their industry and their customers *love* their floral pieces and arrangements. As a wedding florist, one of their specialty arrangements is naturally the bridal bouquet. Now, as is tradition in many weddings, the bride tosses her bouquet towards the unmarried women who try to catch it. This is a special moment, but many brides would love to keep their bridal bouquet as well.

So what does my client do? They don't tell the bride, but after the wedding, they give her a brand new, identical bridal bouquet! She doesn't know this is coming at all, so *it's a total surprise.* This can be a very powerful experience. As you can well imagine, many a bride has gone on to tell her friends about my client and the special gift they received. Find a way to do something surprising and inspirational like this. You'll be glad you did.

So when it comes to customer appreciation, I've got three keys I want you to take away from this chapter:

1. **Find a way to make them feel special**
2. **Create a client rewards program**
3. **Surprise and delight them**

Again, sit down with your team and think outside the box on this one. Find a way to own this and make it a core part of who you are as a business and how you interact with customers.

Chapter 43

CUSTOMER MEASUREMENT

This chapter is short and sweet, but also critical. Just like every other area on your bike, we need to measure your efforts with your customers—the people cheering you on and lifting your business up. *You have an obligation to make sure you're tracking and measuring your improvement here.* If you don't, *how will you know you're getting better?* It's a theme throughout this book: *this can't be a gut thing.* This is way too important to leave to chance.

You've got to measure your relationship with your customers because, as we covered earlier, *they won't tell you when you're doing poorly.* They are not likely to volunteer the information that the person across town is outperforming you. You know what they'll do though? *They'll simply leave.* You're not going to know it until you haven't seen them for a while, but they will just leave you for a competitor with a new store, activity, or service.

But you won't know it until you say, "Hmmm... I wonder what happened to so-and-so?" But by then, they're already gone. Someone else is already making them feel important, showing them how much more they appreciate them than you. So you must measure where you're at with customers because that's the only way you'll ever know. I've got three pointers for you on measuring customer relationships:

#1: JUST DO IT

A good way to start is by applying the *Nike* methodology, "Just do it." Just start tracking how you're doing with customers and how much they appreciate it. All that means is *find a way to have quantifiable data and start tracking it.* So again, *"Just do it."*

But don't go overboard or get ahead of yourself. This is an area where slow and steady wins. This isn't about putting in a burst of effort, going over-the-top with something fancy, spending a lot of money, and hoping your customers appreciate it. No, this is about *steady, consistent measurement of behavior around your customers and feedback from them about your business, team, product, or service.* So don't go overboard. Slow and steady on this one.

#2: SET A GOAL FOR IMPROVEMENT

Once you begin measuring, *set a goal for improvement.* That is, once you've gotten feedback through your system once or twice and have started to get a sense of where you really are, *set a target.* Don't try to go from a 6 out of 10 to a 9.5 out of 10 in six months. No, this is not some sort of rapid improvement system. This is about *consistent, steady improvement.*

So if you're at 6 out of 10 right now, set a goal of 6.5 or 7 out of 10. Once you get that, set another reasonable goal—just like Lawrence of Arabia. Set a goal and let your team know what you're thinking, where you want to go, and what feedback you will be tracking. Make it clear to them where you want to improve so you are all on the same page.

Make sure you give your team a chance to get on board with this. In fact, you may want to set up some type of incentive for them to help facilitate this. It's got to be genuine, though. You can't let it be manipulated. But if it's real and they *are* engaged, then they will get it. See that there's something for them in it, and they will lift your business up.

#3: UPDATE YOUR DASHBOARD

Remember your dashboard? Your results tracking tool? I want you to create some dashboard dials to specifically track how your customers feel about you to see how this trends over time.

You're going to need some quantifiable data to chart for this. Hopefully you'll see increases in the key areas as you track and measure. Yes, this is a simple start, but just do it. Just get rolling with it and start measuring your progress.

Once you start going with this, you're going to find many ways you can get better and more creative. You'll come up with more interesting ideas and your customers will become more engaged with you and your team. They're going to think you are a rock star because you're *treating them* like rock stars.

So the key here is making sure you have the graphs and quantifiable data points so you can track trends in order to improve results over time.

SECTION EIGHT

FINANCIAL CONTROLS OVERVIEW

Chapter 44

UNDERSTANDING
FINANCIAL CONTROLS

I n this final section we'll be talking about the financial controls and Key Performance Indicators (KPIs) you need to ensure your business stays on the path to success. These are the brakes and other indicators on your bike—those things you rely upon for solid control over how well your bike is running, how well your business is going.

Imagine you're watching an important basketball game. There's a minute left and the score is tied. Suddenly, the scoreboard goes black. You can't see a thing. The game continues, but you don't know how much time is left, what the score is, who's got how many fouls, who has timeouts left, and you never know when the game ends.

How would that feel? Is that a game you want to watch? Are you going to be excited and engaged, or are you going to lose interest and be frustrated? The scenario I just described, trying to compete without even knowing the score, is sadly how many business owners run their business. Without a scoreboard, how can they know if they are winning or losing? They don't even know how much time they have to make any big moves.

You need a scoreboard to know when to make adjustments, which means you need financial controls and KPIs. Know this—your business is no toy. No, your business is a bike built for speed, and to go fast, you're going to need some controls and gauges, you're going to need a scoreboard.

DISCIPLINE IS ONLY HALF OF THE EQUATION

I've already shared a bit about my dad's finances. It's not something I am proud of, nor was he. He didn't have a bank account for most of the time he ran his business. He literally lived hand to mouth, day to day. That's no way to run a railroad. That's for sure.

And at the time, I didn't know it could or should be different. In fact, it wasn't until I began working on my degree in Accounting that I understood the purpose, power and necessity of documents like P&L statements, balance sheets, cash flow forecasts and budgets.

My dad did keep good records, but they were all hand-written on his big chief tablets. His life's work was in those notebooks. Day in and day out, he maintained the rhythm. At the end of each day, he would reconcile his ledger, listing the jobs completed, fees paid, and amounts still owed. The point I want you to see is that no amount of discipline or hard work is going to pay off with your financial controls and KPIs without the right knowledge and awareness.

That's the goal of this section—to give you the awareness and knowledge you need to apply your own discipline around financial management. My dad only had part of the equation here, which is not enough. I want you to have the full equation, so you'll get far different results in your business.

Chapter 45

FINANCIAL PLAN & MODEL

Without financial indicators, you won't know what to do or be able to make decisions with certainty. That's the goal here—setting you up to be able to make good decisions because you're looking at the right financials and metrics. You need to be able to see what's going on so you can easily predict the future to make great decisions that will accelerate your business forward faster and faster.

You've heard it said that business is a game. If business is a game you intend to win, then obviously you should keep score. A big part of what you need to do to keep score in business is have a plan, or metrics, or something to measure yourself against to know if you're winning or losing, whether you're gaining ground or falling behind.

Think about other areas of your life for a minute. Do you take your family on vacation without a plan? Of course not! How much more important is it that you plan out what goes on financially in your business? I think you know—it's critically important.

(YEAR) OPERATING BUDGET

	JAN	FEB	ETC.	TOTAL	BUDGET
REVENUES					
GROSS SALES					
DIRECT EXPENSES					
COST OF GOODS SOLD					
GROSS MARGIN					
%					
OPERATING EXPENSES					
TOTAL					
NET OPERATING PROFIT					
%					
RETAINED EARNINGS					
CUM RETAINED EARNINGS					
BREAK EVEN AFTER					

STEP #1: ESTABLISH A BUDGET

The first action item is to *establish a budget for your business.* Look at the budget template I've included with this chapter. It's fairly simple to understand. Let's step through it very briefly:

Section One: Revenues

At the very top, put your revenues. If they come from different sources, areas, or activities within your business, include that. You may have multiple revenue sources. If so, list them separately so you can see which are growing and which are not.

Allocate amounts based on each month. Think about how you intend for your revenue to flow from month to month and do so for different categories of revenue.

Section Two: Direct Expenses Or Cost Of Goods Sold

Next is your direct expenses or cost of goods sold. These are expenses that relate *directly* to the selling of your product or service. This specifically excludes overhead. So, no rent, no internet or phone bill, no fuel expenses. All you want here are the costs associated with the production or delivery of your product or service. This includes direct production labor, raw materials, freight costs, direct supervision, etc.

When you subtract your cost of goods sold from your revenue, you are left with your **gross profit** or **gross margin**. That *gross margin* is what you have left over to cover the operating expenses in your business.

Section Three: Itemized Operating Expenses

The third category of your budget is a listing of your business's itemized operating expenses. Be *as specific as you can possibly be here.* Lay them all out—your telephone bill, your web charges, marketing expenses, rent, any loan payments, and any other expenses you regularly incur like membership fees and bank charges. These are all *operating expenses* as opposed to a cost of goods sold.

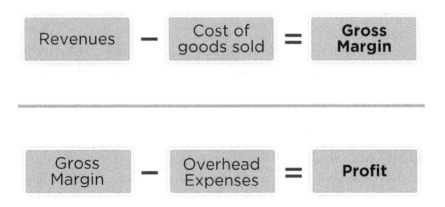

What's left after you take itemized operating expenses away from your gross margin is your **net operating profit**. So establish a budget. You can find other templates online. Just search for budgets and you'll find many different versions you can use.

STEP #2: UNDERSTAND YOUR BREAK-EVEN ANALYSIS

After you have a budget set, *make sure you have a clear understanding of your break-even analysis.* A break-even analysis is simply a way to look at the dollars visually. I've included a small matrix to make this clearer:

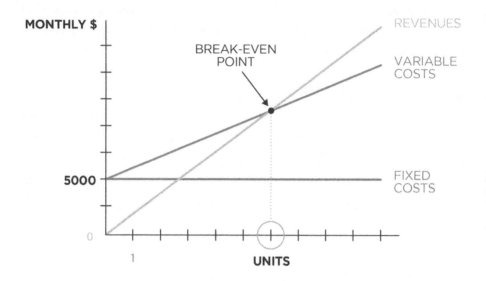

As you look at this, notice the vertical, or *Y*-axis represents **dollar amounts**, and the horizontal, or *X*-axis, is **units**. So we're relating dollars received to units produced—either units of product or of a service, whatever works for your business.

Plot Your Fixed Monthly Costs Line

Now, as you draw your own chart, first draw a line that represents your monthly fixed operating costs (this is in red above). These are costs that do not change whether you produce 1 or 1000 units. That's why they are called *fixed.* You'll see the fixed costs are $5000 in the matrix above. This red line represents *monthly fixed expenses.*

Plot Your Cost Of Goods Or Variable Cost On A Per Unit Basis

Next, break down your cost of goods sold on a per unit basis. This reflects the cost of producing each unit you sell. This amount is additive to your fixed cost. So start at your fixed cost line (the red line), and then create *a variable cost line* (in blue). Keep in mind the following:

- Variable costs are simply those incurred every time you produce or sell a unit.

- If you have no variable costs, this amount is zero. So your total cost of running your business would simply be your fixed costs.

- The slope of the variable cost line will represent the incremental, or variable, costs you incur as you produce more units.

Plot A Revenue Line

The green line on the graph, as indicated, is the *revenue line*. This line starts at zero and goes up every time you sell a unit. Now, obviously you sell a unit for a certain dollar amount, but you might have an average dollar sale if you sell different types of units. However you track it, the more units you sell, the higher your revenues climb.

Identify Your Break Even Point

Now here's the key: **find the place where your revenue line crosses your variable cost line, this is your breakeven point.** This is where your revenue = your fixed costs + your variable costs. Simply draw a line down from that point to find out how many units you must sell to breakeven each month.

It is important to know your break-even chart in detail. Keep this clearly in mind because it represents your business's profit opportunity. It's the point where profit begins to exist in your business, where your revenue line eclipses both fixed and variable costs.

Once your chart is built, refresh it again and again—particularly if you have a seasonal business where your units sold may be lower than your break-even point. This will let you anticipate the down cycles so you can avoid spending more money than you're earning.

Do this first on a monthly basis, then as you get more sophisticated consider calculating this on a weekly basis. Ultimately, you may even do it on a daily or hourly basis. Your breakeven chart is a *powerful* visual that can help generate more profit in your business.

STEP #3: BUILD A CASH-FLOW FORECAST

With your break-even analysis in hand, it's easy for you to *build your cash flow forecast*. This is a monthly report similar to your budget, as you can see in the following image:

CASH FLOW PROJECTION

		MONTH 1	MONTH 2	MONTH 3	MONTH etc.	TOTAL
Business Name						
12 Month Period						
Cash Flow Projection						
CASH ON HAND		0.00	0.00	0.00	0.00	0.00
CASH RECEIPTS		0.00	0.00	0.00	0.00	0.00
TOTAL CASH RECEIPTS		0.00	0.00	0.00	0.00	0.00
TOTAL CASH AVAILABLE		0.00	0.00	0.00	0.00	0.00
CASH PAID OUT		0.00	0.00	0.00	0.00	0.00
TOTAL CASH PAID OUT		0.00	0.00	0.00	0.00	0.00
CASH POSITION		0.00	0.00	0.00	0.00	0.00

The difference here is that you are tracking the **sources** and **uses** of your cash. The top part of the form represents *your sources of cash or revenue*. These would be sales as well as any other revenue sources or recurring monthly incomes. Include these in the sources of cash.

The section below that shows how you use that cash. Here you track the things that *take cash out of* your business. This excludes depreciation and other non-cash items because you need to know on a month-by-month basis whether your plan or budget will allow you to *(1) generate cash* or *(2) use cash*. Remember, most companies go out of business because they do not forecast their cash needs. Make this a priority to ensure you're successful.

STEP #4: ADOPT A PROFIT-FIRST MINDSET

Next, adopt a profit-first mindset. To help with that, I recommend the book *Profit First* by Mike Michalowicz. Let me briefly go over Mike's very insightful book:

- **Step #1: Pay the Profit to Your Business First:** This is a very intentional and powerful way to examine the way your business finances ought to flow. Another way of saying this is, identify what kind of profit you want from your business first. Create a profit account so that every time you make a sale, some percentage of that sale goes into your profit account. This way you pay the profit to your business first.

- **Step #2: Pay Yourself a Salary:** Next, you pay yourself a salary as the business owner. This makes sure you're getting paid for the effort of ownership you put into the business. So first is your profit. Second is your owner's compensation.

- **Step #3: Set Aside Money for Taxes:** Next, set aside some money from that sale to cover your taxes because that's an obligation that you have to the government that you can't let slide. Make sure you have a tax account set up so that some portion of each dollar of revenue that comes in goes to your taxes.

- **Step #4: Use the Remainder as Your Business Expense Account:** What you're left with is *your expense account*. If you run your business within that expense amount, you can rest easy knowing your business will be profitable.

I know we covered a lot, but having a good handle on your finances is critically important to being successful in business in the long term. Get this right and everything else will work out nicely. But if you do everything else and don't focus here, no matter how great your intentions, you won't be able to last because you need to be profitable to make it work over the long haul.

This is the beginning of getting a firm, hard grip on your handlebars and brakes of your bike so that you know when to pull on one or the other. When you look at these indicators, you'll know what's going on and how your bike will respond.

TUNE-UP TIP: Here's one to think about: many, many business owners get stuck because during the times when they generate extra cash, *they are unaware they are doing so!* On top of this, they fail to anticipate lean months ahead when they'll need that extra cash. Instead of being prepared, these owners unknowingly burn cash down they need to get through tough times. So here's your tip: *store up during your times of harvest to get you through the winter.*

Chapter 46

FINANCIAL METRICS

N
ow, it's time to start talking *financial metrics*. We've got a plan already, something to work from to chart your success. The next step is simply tracking what happens in your business.

Metrics simply means *tracking and measuring the activities in your business that affect your financial results*. Here's a reality that many business owners don't understand: the finances, the actual dollars in & dollars out, are simply *a result of activities in your business*.

Think about that for a minute. The activities you do are what drives your financial outcomes. So let's move back upstream and track the significant activities in your business that drive your financial results. Here are some examples to get you started:

1. **Lead Generation.** Ask yourself, *how many leads am I generating? What's my cost to generate each lead?* If you track your cost per lead and number of leads generated, you will begin to know *your actual client-acquisition cost.*
2. **Product Costs.** You could also track your cost to produce a product or deliver a particular service.

3. **Support Costs.** If you have a team of people supporting a large number of customers, you could track your costs per customer to provide support.

This is just a start. There are many activities you can track and translate into financial results that indicate success or failure. Here's a three-step process to get you started:

STEP #1: RESEARCH YOUR INDUSTRY

First, *research your industry.* You have to know its norms, so spend some time specifically examining and researching it. *What standards does your industry typically measure?*

- If you work as a consultant, one of those industry standards is *utilization rate.* How much of your time is billable? Is it 75%, 80% or 85%? There's a norm or standard for your industry. *Determine that standard.*
- If you're in manufacturing, there's a cost of goods sold as a % of revenues model. Your target gross profit may need to be around 55-60% when it is actually in the 45-50% range.

But to know *any* of this, must know your industry's norms. Every industry is different and unique. What are your specific industry norms? You'll need to research what typically is measured in your industry in order to have standards that you could replicate. Research and gain insight into what others are doing. Look for those doing it well, those you would consider to be best in class in your industry and model what they do.

STEP #2: LEARN WHAT DRIVES VALUE IN YOUR INDUSTRY

Next, *know what drives business value in your industry.* Learn the specific indicators that determine the market value of a business in your industry. Again, this is different for every industry, but there are typically one or two indicators that those who are interested in purchasing businesses look for to determine if it's a good investment. This may be debt/equity ratio, or a target growth rate percentage for the industry. You must learn what those indicators are so you can factor them into your thinking and planning.

As you determine what these primary indicators of value are, make sure you're measuring the activities that will drive those value indicators. You're not measuring things just for fun. You're doing this *to track the things that matter most in your industry.* You want to Track the things that will generate value in your business so that later on, when you decide to transfer or sell your business, it will be worth far more than it is now. That's always the big goal, so you must know what those value indicators are for your industry.

STEP #3: BUILD A FINANCIAL DASHBOARD

Once these first two are set, you're in a position to build *a financial dashboard.* We've talked about it many times already, so this is simply putting together all the pieces.

When it comes to how you track this for your dashboard, you have some options on tools that are available to you. Look on the web, shop around, and find a dashboard tool that works for you. There are *many* options available. Some are pre-formatted, make inputting data simple, and will easily create charts and graphs to show you visually where your business is at.

If you can adopt the mindset of consistently tracking, documenting, measuring, and sharing the data with your entire team, you will see noticeable improvements in how well your business performs. *This is powerful for your business* because you will make data-based decisions *that will drive your business forward faster and make it stronger.*

So do these three things: (1) research your industry, (2) learn what drives value in your industry, and then (3) take time to build your financial metrics. Make sure you do everything you can to ensure you're tracking the right metrics for your business and industry.

Start simple. Don't overwhelm your team or go too big at first. Start by finding 1–3 metrics you want to track. You can always add more later. Once you get going, things will become clearer. With 6+ months of data, you'll feel incredibly empowered and be so glad you did this.

Chapter 47

KEY PERFORMANCE INDICATORS

N ow it's time to talk about the other indicators in your business. We've already mentioned them a little, I'm talking about your *Key Performance Indicators*. KPIs are indicators used as predictors of future success. These are a way for us to look into the crystal ball and see what's going to happen to your business in the future. We'll focus on the things that *precede* a sale or the generation of revenue.

The first step is figuring out what KPIs will be important to your business. This should be fairly simple. To help, I want to give you some examples:

LEAD GENERATION

A good place to start is, *how many leads are you generating?* Each week, each day, you're collecting new prospects. You're using your marketing strategies to connect with your ideal prospects. How many new potential customers are you connecting with each week? Track and measure that number weekly so you can see whether you are generating more or fewer leads over time. Knowing this can help you predict what will happen with your business in the future.

To get more detailed, track leads by source. *Where are your leads coming from? Are they coming from a Google AdWords campaign? Are they coming from a direct mail piece? Are you meeting leads at networking groups or because of associations you are in?* Ask yourself, *where are my leads coming from?*

Maybe they're all from referral sources or perhaps referrals are falling off. If you know this, then you can ask, *why?* You can even get more sophisticated by tracking each specific marketing campaign which will allow you to know the effectiveness of one marketing campaign over another.

You should also track your *cost per lead.* Find out how much you spend to generate a lead. How powerful would it be to know if you are putting your resources in the right place to maximize the bang for your marketing buck? Again, this is an indicator of future success because if your cost per lead goes down, you can generate more leads without increasing your spending—something you definitely want to do.

CONVERSION RATE

Another KPI you should measure is *how well you convert leads into customers.* If you generate 10 leads, can you convert one of them, meaning a 10% conversion rate? Are you converting 2 out of every 10, or 20%? Tracking this on a daily or weekly basis, particularly if you have a sales team, lets you see how effective your sales process is and where improvements are needed.

Once you know this, you can make changes to your sales process to ensure you incrementally increase conversion rate. This also helps you ensure success by telling you how many leads you must generate to hit your revenue targets at your current conversion rate.

SALES METRICS

Another KPI to track is *average dollar amount per sale.* When people buy from you, what's the average ticket price that they're purchasing? Is their average ticket price $10? For example, if you run a sub shop and your average ticket price is $9.95, maybe you can train your staff and move that up to $10.50 or even $11.00? But the first step is being able to track so you know how well you are doing and can make changes to increase your average ticket price in the future.

Consider tracking actual sales per day. That way you can determine if Monday is better than Tuesday, etc., and start to see what days of the week need more or less staff on the schedule. It helps you know whether you should reduce costs or increase activity accordingly.

You can also track your types of sales. For example, what are your custom-order sales? What about customers buying off the floor, or online sales? Identify and measure each type of sale you currently make.

PRODUCTION METRICS

You should also track several production or manufacturing metrics. What are your total production costs per unit and/or per hour? In other words, look into efficiency measurements as potential KPIs to predict future success. Are you getting better at production? More efficient? More effective? Metrics will paint the picture for you.

We've covered several examples. I know your business and industry will have some specific things to keep in mind beyond what we just discussed. If you need to, pull your team together and ask them to help with this. Once you have your KPIs picked out, I have two final thoughts for you:

1. **Track your KPIs at least weekly**. Use a weekly metric as your longest period to go between measurements. This gives you *52 opportunities to collect data throughout the year.* If you do it just once a month, you only have 12 data points. That's not enough. So use 52, that's once a week as a minimum, to measure your KPIs.

2. **Post your tracked KPI results in graphic format where everybody can see them.** This will inspire people when they start to see trends. Conversely, they'll be alarmed if they see the negative trends and help you find solutions to get back on track. Make sure to post your results every week.

TUNE-UP TIP: A few final thoughts on KPIs: (1) pick the ones that are right for you, and (2) start with just a handful. You can always add to these later just like you can on the financial side. But start with a few so that you can get used to looking forward in your business and predicting the future. This is one sure way to make that future a lot brighter. Do this and you'll be on your way to having a powerful business.

Chapter 48

BUSINESS DASHBOARD

Wе've discussed measurement in virtually every section of the book. From the front and rear wheels, to the seat and even your racing team and fans. We've continually talked about how to measure the results of your efforts.

I hope it's now clear to you how *every aspect of your bike or business affords you the opportunity to measure.* Remember, measurement is the only way you're going to know whether you're getting better. So you must: (1) track data, (2) put that data into some graphic format and (3) use it to inform your decisions.

If you want to go fast in business, *you must have a solid dashboard.* If you intend for your business to grow fast and to grow big, then you've got to put some disciplined effort behind this.

This is a critical piece for your business, one that you alone can do. *You set the vision, the standards, the processes, and you measure the activities.* What gets measured *matters.* People will know you by what you measure and say is important. Before we wrap up here, I have three fundamental thoughts to put a bow on this discussion:

#1: START SIMPLE

The first thought is this: *whatever you do in this area (as in every other area of your business) start simple.* Don't get too complicated. Don't try to leap tall buildings the first time you jump. It will simply distract and discourage everyone. If you make the process too complicated, *people will stop doing it.*

This is a good indicator you're going too fast, making it too difficult. You'll know this is the case when your people find reasons not to do it. So start simple and be additive. Just start *somewhere.* Let everybody know this is a non-negotiable piece and explain how you are going to track activities, post results, and keep score. Let them know you're just going to get more and more deliberate and comprehensive as you go. They'll see the results as you go along.

#2: MAKE BUSINESS DECISIONS BASED ON THE DATA YOU TRACK

Second fundamental: *make decisions in your business based on the data you track.* It's a mistake to make decisions from the gut, even though many people insist on doing this.

I get why people trust their gut, but what's more powerful and impactful is *looking at the data to help make the right decisions.* And if you don't have the data, perhaps maybe you ought to defer on this particular decision until you take some time to collect it.

The goal here is not to slow down progress, but rather to make good decisions. I want you to be a decision maker who always asks the question, "What is the data telling me to do? What's our trend showing? And what does that mean in terms of making decisions?"

#3: DELEGATE RESPONSIBILITY FOR THE DASHBOARD

Another principal: delegate the responsibility for this. Don't try to do it all yourself. Yes, do set the template, methodology, and mindset, but don't do all the rest. Delegate this to your team.

If you require them to do it, *they'll own it*. They'll enjoy being responsible for the tracking, measuring, posting, and other ongoing activities because they're going to find personal satisfaction in the progress they see just as you will. *Share that satisfaction with your team.* Let them own it and be responsible for it. Let them take the initiative to coordinate meeting deadlines and get the data uploaded and the graphs refreshed. This will be very powerful.

#4: HOLD PEOPLE ACCOUNTABLE

And a final thought here: *use this to hold your people accountable.* Hold them accountable for the results in the business. Pretty simple, right? Well that's what it's all about—getting them to run your business so well that you don't even have to be there each and every day.

This is all about the powerful toolset you now have for measuring your business—*your dashboard.* I hope you've got some clear ideas on how to make this work for your business. Now, go out there and make it happen!

CONCLUSION

Chapter 49

PARTING THOUGHTS

I sincerely hope you have found this book to be helpful in your journey to becoming a better business owner. Writing this book has been both enjoyable and therapeutic for me.

I have enjoyed reminiscing about my dad and sharing many of the lessons I have learned from him. The more I reflect on his experience as a business owner, the more I can recognize the struggles, challenges and sometimes conflicting situations that business owners find themselves in today.

While it has been several years since my dad was actively working his business, it is clear to me that many of the issues are still the same. Technologies have changed, access to information has changed, and the ways we communicate with our customers is far different than is was back in my dad's days. But still, many of the fundamentals of running a good business have not changed one bit.

SEEK WISE COUNSEL

One of those fundamentals that has not changed, and in fact has become even more important in business today, is the idea of surrounding yourself with many advisors. Beginning with the teachings in the Bible, wise men and women have always surrounded themselves with many wise counselors. (Proverbs 15:22)

My dad didn't practice this very well, but he often talked about how important it was. This was one of the areas where he gave good advice, but didn't necessarily live out his own advice in his business. I don't think this was because of pride as much as it was from simply being overwhelmed. Dad found himself so busy IN his business that he rarely took the time to work ON his business—let alone take time to sit and discuss it with someone who could give him wise business advice.

Don't be like my dad in this regard. Do what is necessary to surround yourself with good, informed advisors. The fact that you've read this book is an indication that you are following this advice. Good for you!

SHARE THE GIFT

Now, the best gift you could give me (and my dad) is for you to not only put these business practices in place in your business, but to also share this book with a friend.

As I mentioned earlier, my dad's dream of building a successful, sustainable business never came to fruition. But my dream and my goal is to leave a legacy to my dad by sharing these lessons from a window washer with as many small business owners as I possibly can in hopes that their dreams CAN and WILL come true.

I know that my dad would be proud if just one business owner found his story to be both compelling and convicting and as a result, changed their business for the better and achieved the success they desired and deserved. If that's you, then the efforts of this work have been well worth it. If you know of someone who could use inspiration and motivation to begin their journey towards building a successful business, please share this with them and our mission will be fulfilled.

No matter what, thank you for taking this journey with me. If there is anything I can do to personally help you with your business, don't hesitate to reach out and ask.

I wish you success and fulfillment with your business. May you be blessed so that you can share those blessings with others who you encounter along your path towards success and significance.

Epilogue

WHERE TO GO
FROM HERE...

W e touched on so many topics and authors throughout our journey together in this book that I wanted to leave you with a list of additional readings I recommend for more information on the topics we covered in each Section.

SECTION ONE: YOU AS A BUSINESS OWNER
- *Success Principles* by Jack Canfield
- *Secrets of the Millionaire Mind* by T. Harv Eker
- *Getting Things Done* by David Allen
- *Eat That Frog* by Brian Tracy
- *Total Leadership* by Stewart Friedman
- *Mojo* by Marshall Goldsmith
- *The 4-Hour Workweek* by Timothy Ferris

SECTION TWO: THE HANDLEBARS OF YOUR BUSINESS
- *Start With Why* by Simon Sinek
- *Blue Ocean Strategy* by W. Chan Kim
- *The Greatest Business Decisions of All Time* by Vern Harnish

- *The Boy Who Harnessed the Wind* by B. Mealer
- *Making Ideas Happen* by Scott Belsky

SECTION THREE: THE STRUCTURE & FRAME OF YOUR BUSINESS
- *Entrance* by William Whitehurst
- *Exit* by Alexander Vantarakis
- *The E-Myth Revisited* by Michael Gerber
- *It's OK to Be the Boss* by Bruce Tulgan

SECTION FOUR: WINNING CUSTOMERS
- *Launch* by Jeff Walker
- *David and Goliath* by Malcolm Gladwell
- *A Whole New Mind* by Daniel Pink
- *Permission Marketing* by Seth Godin
- *Guerilla Marketing* by Jay Levinson
- *Jab, Jab, Jab, Right Hook* by Gary Vaynerchuk
- *Crush It!* By Gary Vaynerchuk
- *Tribes* by Seth Godin
- *Free Publicity* by Jeff Crilley
- *What Would Google Do?* by Jeff Jarvis
- *The Sales Bible* by Jeffrey Gitomer
- *Pitch Anything* by Oren Klaff
- *Selling the Wheel* by Jeff Cox
- *Marketing Metrics* by Paul Ferris

SECTION FIVE: SERVING CUSTOMERS
- *Built to Serve* by Dan Sanders
- *The Design of Everyday Things* by Don Norman
- *Thinking in Systems* by Donella Meadows
- *The Kaizen Way* by Robert Mauer
- *Rework* by Jason Fried
- *The Goal* by Eli Goldratt

SECTION SIX: BUILDING A WINNING TEAM

- *Delivering Happiness* by Tony Hsieh
- Zappos Culture Book
- *Hiring the Best* by Martin Yate
- *Drive* by Daniel Pink
- *Flight of the Buffalo* by James Belasco
- *The Energy Bus* by Jon Gordon
- *Leaders Eat Last* by Simon Sinek
- *First Break All the Rules* by Marcus Buckingham
- *Now, Discover Your Strengths* by Marcus Buckingham

SECTION SEVEN: UNDERSTANDING YOUR CUSTOMERS

- *Raving Fans* by Ken Blanchard
- *Secret Service* by John DiJulius
- *What Clients Love* by Harry Beckwith
- *The Starbucks Experience* by Joseph Mischelli

SECTION EIGHT: FINANCIAL CONTROLS

- *Profit First* by Mike Michalowicz
- *Keys to the Vault* by Keith Cunningham
- *Financial Intelligence* for Entrepreneurs by Karen Berman
- *Turning Numbers into Knowledge* by Jonathan Koomey
- *Think Like a Freak* by Stephen Levitt

A free eBook edition is available with the purchase of this book.

To claim your free eBook edition:

1. Download the Shelfie app.
2. Write your name in upper case in the box.
3. Use the Shelfie app to submit a photo.
4. Download your eBook to any device.

Shelfie

A free eBook edition is available
with the purchase of this print book.

CLEARLY PRINT YOUR NAME ABOVE IN UPPER CASE

Instructions to claim your free eBook edition:
1. Download the Shelfie app for Android or iOS
2. Write your name in **UPPER CASE** above
3. Use the Shelfie app to submit a photo
4. Download your eBook to any device

Print & Digital Together Forever.

Snap a photo   Free eBook   Read anywhere

Morgan James makes all of our titles available
through the Library for All Charity Organizations.

www.LibraryForAll.org

Printed in the USA
CPSIA information can be obtained
at www.ICGtesting.com
JSHW022216140824
68134JS00018B/1087

9 781683 500575